The FAMILY-
FRIENDLY
CHURCH

The FAMILY-FRIENDLY CHURCH

|||||||||||||||||||

Richard D. Dobbins

Creation House
Altamonte Springs, Florida

Copyright © 1989 by Richard D. Dobbins
All rights reserved
Printed in the United States of America
Library of Congress Catalog Card Number: 88-64194
International Standard Book Number: 0-88419-228-8

Creation House
Strang Communications Company
190 N. Westmonte Drive
Altamonte Springs, FL 32714
(407) 869-5005

Unless otherwise noted, all Scripture quotations are taken
from the Holy Bible, New International Version; copyright
© 1973, 1978, 1984 by International Bible Society; used by
permission. Scripture quotations marked KJV are from the
King James Version of the Bible; used by permission. The
Scripture quotation marked NBV is taken from The Modern
Language Bible: The Berkeley Version in Modern English;
copyright © 1945, 1959, 1969 by Zondervan Publishing
House; used by permission.

To my loving wife, Dolores

Acknowledgments

We are most grateful for the many contributions that have made this book possible. Special thanks is due Mrs. Lila Pond for sharing with us personal insights into the blended family experience. Carol Adams has been a constant source of help in library research and editing. Lynne Ternent, my secretary for more than twenty-five years, has kept my schedule free so that I could work on the manuscript.

Special thanks are also due the many pastors who participated in our first seminar on this subject. They helped me keep my eyes on the practical needs of the local church.

Finally, I would like to thank my daughter Sharon for her patience and persistent pursuit of this project with me. Her insights and editorial skills have been an invaluable resource.

Contents

Preface

Sooner or later, we all learn that "experience is the best teacher." As the apostle Paul reminds us in his letter to the Romans, "we glory in tribulations also: knowing that tribulation worketh patience; and patience, experience; and experience, hope: and hope maketh not ashamed; because the love of God is shed abroad in our hearts by the Holy Ghost which is given unto us" (Rom. 5:3-5, KJV).

Currently I am looking back on a lifetime of varied experience: forty-three years of marriage, four years in evangelistic work, twenty-six years in the pastorate and twenty-three years in Christian counseling. Through these involvements I have shared in much tribulation, developed more patience than I ever dreamed I could and accumulated a wealth of experience in family and church relations.

Because I have seen the Lord do so much in my own family and in the families of others who have looked to Him for help, I have great hope for the future of the American family. But this hope is anchored firmly in my conviction that the family of God must become a surrogate family for those whose families are broken and, at the same time, must remain a strong source of spiritual support for those whose families are still intact. The church of the twenty-first century must be deeply committed to ministering to family needs. I am convinced that without a strong spiritual foundation the traditional family will not survive.

Storms of materialism, humanism, hedonism and self-serving narcissism are beating against the weakened foundations of America's families as they are crowded into amoral and impersonal megaplexes. The backlash of these storms is seeping into our churches, resulting in more and more Christian families suffering from such problems as sexual promiscuity, adultery, unwanted pregnancies, substance abuse and divorce.

Although my heart is hopeful, honest reflection on my experience with thousands of hurting Christians caught in the wake of these storms reveals an urgent need in the family of God. If Christians are going to rise above the swelling tide of a morally decaying society, we must become more thoughtful and caring toward each other. We must recognize that God has called us into a new relationship with Him *and with each other*.

Being "born again" indeed signifies the beginning of this new family relationship. But it is only the beginning.

We evangelicals are great spiritual midwives, but our skills in nurturing the "newborn" and helping them develop into mature saints disciplined in the faith are substantially lacking. Our churches are full of people who need more than a new-birth experience. If these people are going to grow and mature in their Christian life, they must find people in the church whose prayers and practical love will show them the way. They need the compassionate care of a loving spiritual family.

This book is written to help pastors turn their congregations into communities of believing families willing to care for their brothers and sisters in Christ. From pastoral experience, I know how difficult it is for some people in the church to accept change. Therefore, many of my suggestions involve areas of church life over which the pastor has undisputed authority. Others supplement, rather than supplant, the traditional approach to worship and Christian education. Most of the suggestions call for supplemental care groups organized around specific needs and for an enrichment of the electives offered in the Christian education department. We have extensively researched recent evangelical publications to provide additional background materials for implementing various phases of the programs we suggest. These are listed in the suggested readings following each chapter. (Since these materials represent a wide range of evangelical opinion it cannot be assumed that the author endorses every viewpoint presented.)

For many of the ideas presented here I am indebted

to pastors of dynamic churches who have been kind enough to invite me to be their pulpit guest. I am also indebted to the scores of people who have told me about the ministries they wish were available in their local churches.

Few if any churches will be able to use all of the suggestions. But I pray that each pastor who reads these pages will discover ways to extend the compassionate, healing ministry of his church to needs not presently being addressed. The church must provide a caring community that will help broken families restore a sense of healing and wholeness to their lives.

I hope you will find in this book biblically sound and practical ways to transform your congregation into a caring community of believing families.

What Is Happening to the Family?

The American family is changing. No sophisticated study is needed to reveal this fact. Parents of today's elementary school children can confirm this reality simply by recalling the television families of their childhood and comparing them with those of today. "Leave It to Beaver," "I Love Lucy" and "Father Knows Best" have been replaced by "thirtysomething," "Family Ties" and "Dallas."

Of course, some could argue that most of these changes are for the better since they reflect a higher standard of living for the average American family.

However, the standard of living is not the only thing that has been rising during this time. The rates of adultery, divorce, teenage sexual promiscuity and pregnancy, violent crime among the young, homosexuality and drug abuse are escalating. And the increasing numbers of single-parent families, working mothers with preschool children, runaway children, and old people living alone remind us of the terrible price our affluence is exacting. Today's family is struggling to survive; the church is struggling to save it. If we are to succeed in our mission to restore the family, we must have the courage to challenge creatively our traditional methods and allow the Holy Spirit to help us define new ways of ministering to the modern family.

As alarming and disheartening as the struggle of the modern family may be, it is not unprecedented. The church faced a strikingly similar situation in first-century Rome.

The Family in First-Century Rome

By the dawn of the first century, the Roman empire had reached its cultural apex. Many Romans were enjoying the creaturely benefits of a world economic power—comfort, pleasure, education and wealth. However, during this time when the emerging Western world was feeling the sting of Caesar's taxes, materialism was exacting another kind of toll from the heart of Roman society.

The first-century Roman family was disintegrating under the ponderous weight of unparalleled prosperity. Single-parent households, childless marriages, common-law marriages, divorces and remarriages were commonplace. Mechanical and chemical contraception, abortion, sexual promiscuity and homosexuality abounded.

Historian Will Durant writes of these times in *Caesar and Christ* (Simon and Schuster):

> Once the Romans had been precipitated into parentage by the impetus of sex, and lured to it by anxiety for the post-mortem care of their graves; now the upper and middle classes had learned to separate sex from parentage, and were skeptical about the afterworld.
>
> Marriage, which had once been a lifelong economic union, was now among a hundred thousand Romans a passing adventure of no great spiritual significance, a loose contract for the mutual provision of physiological conveniences of political aid.

This was the cultural context in which the early Christian church developed. This was the morally decaying world Christ came to redeem.

Jesus Came to Redeem the Family

Jesus came to redeem and strengthen family ties. The image of Jesus as God's Passover Lamb in John 1:36 and Revelation 13:8 symbolizes the ultimate and intimate redemption of God's family through His own Son. As you may recall, the Passover is an annual feast designed by God to remind Jewish families of the divine protection given to their firstborn the night God sent the death angel to deliver them from bondage in Egypt.

But Christ's message of family redemption was not

restricted to the Jewish community; it was extended to the Gentiles as well. Remember the promise Paul and Silas gave the Philippian jailer? "Believe in the Lord Jesus, and you will be saved—you and your household" (Acts 16:31).

The Bible is replete with guidelines constructed to protect and strengthen the family. For example, New Testament writers urge Christian couples to avoid divorce and reconcile their differences. Even when believers are married to unbelievers, the family is advised to remain together whenever possible.

> To the married I give this command (not I, but the Lord): A wife must not separate from her husband. But if she does, she must remain unmarried or else be reconciled to her husband. And a husband must not divorce his wife.
>
> To the rest I say this (I, not the Lord): If any brother has a wife who is not a believer and she is willing to live with him, he must not divorce her. And if a woman has a husband who is not a believer and he is willing to live with her, she must not divorce him.
>
> For the unbelieving husband has been sanctified through his wife, and the unbelieving wife has been sanctified through her believing husband. Otherwise your children would be unclean, but as it is, they are holy.
>
> But if the unbeliever leaves, let him do so. A believing man or woman is not bound in such circumstances; God has called us to live in peace. How do you know, wife, whether you

will save your husband?

Or, how do you know, husband, whether you will save your wife? (1 Cor. 7:10-16).

Wives, in the same way be submissive to your husbands so that, if any of them do not believe the word, they may be won over without words by the behavior of their wives, when they see the purity and reverence of your lives. Your beauty should not come from outward adornment, such as braided hair and the wearing of gold jewelry and fine clothes. Instead, it should be that of your inner self, the unfading beauty of a gentle and quiet spirit, which is of great worth in God's sight.

For this is the way the holy women of the past who put their hope in God used to make themselves beautiful. They were submissive to their own husbands, like Sarah, who obeyed Abraham and called him her master. You are her daughters if you do what is right and do not give way to fear.

Husbands, in the same way be considerate as you live with your wives, and treat them with respect as the weaker partner and as heirs with you of the gracious gift of life, so that nothing will hinder your prayers (1 Pet. 3:1-7).

Fathers are to bring their children up in the "training and instruction of the Lord." Parents are not to exasperate their children. When children are young they are to obey their parents. When they grow up they are to honor their father and mother.

> Children, obey your parents in the Lord, for this
> is right. "Honor your father and mother"—which
> is the first commandment with a promise—"that
> it may go well with you and that you may enjoy
> long life on the earth."
> Fathers, do not exasperate your children; in-
> stead, bring them up in the training and instruc-
> tion of the Lord (Eph. 6:1-4).

By showing people how to apply the teachings of
Scripture to their family relationships, the caring
church of the first century redeemed, reconciled and
strengthened families. There is a desperate need for the
church to pursue a similar mission for today's families.

God's Family Is for Everyone

In beginning His ministry Jesus announced His divine
mission to the socially alienated and disenfranchised—
those whose natural families may have been bruised and
broken.

> The Spirit of the Sovereign Lord is on me,
> because the Lord has anointed me to preach good
> news to the poor. He has sent me to bind up the
> brokenhearted, to proclaim freedom for the
> prisoners and release for the prisoners, to pro-
> claim the year of the Lord's favor (Is. 61:1,2a).

What is the gospel or good news Jesus brought to these
whose lives were shattered? He opened to them the
possibility of a new birth into a new family where

God is called Father.

> Yet to all who received him, to those who be-
> lieved in his name, he gave the right to become
> children of God— children born not of natural
> descent, nor of human decision or a husband's
> will, but born of God (John 1:12,13).

Through His life, death and resurrection, Jesus made
it possible for all mankind to become children of God—
to be born into God's family where no one is to be
without love. In fact, Jesus said that the distinguishing
characteristic of God's family is the love each member
has for the others.

> A new command I give you: Love one another.
> As I have loved you, so you must love one
> another. By this all men will know that you are
> my disciples, if you love one another (John
> 13:34,35).

So, in the family of God, healthy families should
discover a love for each other that is greater than they
would naturally have. And those whose natural families
are broken and devoid of love are to find within the family of God the love for which they have longed. As our
heavenly Father wills to shed His love abroad in our
hearts by the Holy Spirit, so we are to extend that love
to each other as brothers and sisters in Christ.

Christian Love Reaches Beyond the Family

Christ came to renew our primary commitment to God
and to strengthen our commitments to each other. But

in admonishing us to love our neighbor as ourselves (see Matt. 19:19), Jesus shifts the focus of our compassion beyond our families or even the family of God. He wants us to care for the needs of those about us who share no more common identity with us than that of fellow members of the human family.

At the heart of the gospel is an all-inclusive community of Christian care. The church of Jesus Christ was born into a culture of broken families and shattered lives. It provided the institutional support and individual care so desperately needed to heal the wounds of these hurting people and enable their families to survive. Salvation means commitment, an eternal commitment of loyalty to God and a lifetime commitment on earth to ''carry each other's burdens, and in this way fulfill the law of Christ'' (see Gal. 6:2). The first-century church took both of these commitments very seriously. Today, our families also need the compassionate concern and commitment that only a caring church can provide.

God Cares for the Family

From the beginning, God has cared for the human family and has longed for us to be in relationship with Him.

This was wonderfully manifest in creation. By a command of His loving will, God called out of chaos an ordered world—a beautiful, life-sustaining habitation prepared for His children.

The human family awakened from the dust into a relationship with God. This relationship was grounded in divine love, loyalty and obedience. The first chapter of Genesis unfolds the beginning of God's relationship with His children:

Then God said, "Let us make man in our image,

in our likeness, and let them rule over the fish of the sea and the birds of the air, over the livestock, over all the earth, and over all the creatures that move along the ground.''

So God created man in his own image, in the image of God he created him; male and female he created them.

God blessed them and said to them, ''Be fruitful and increase in number; fill the earth and subdue it. Rule over the fish of the sea and the birds of the air and over every living creature that moves on the ground'' (Gen. 1:26-28).

What Is a Covenant?

We live in a contract-oriented society. Most Americans know what contracts are. Even in our closest relationships we are extremely interested in making sure we ''get what we bargained for.'' Contracts are defined by *conditions*: ''I will do this *if* you will do that.''

God does not relate to His people contractually. He relates to them on the basis of a special kind of agreement called a *covenant*. In contrast to a contractual relationship, a covenantal relationship requires more than a conditional agreement. According to the *Dictionary of the Bible* (Scribner) a covenant is

> an agreement between two parties in which they pledge themselves in loyalty to one another. It differs from the modern concept of contract in that there is not only an obligation to carry out some specific commitment externally, but a

pledge of loyalty or community of soul. This spiritual content of a covenant, if we can so call it, the inward will which goes beyond outward conformity, is *hesedh* (RSV usually "steadfast love"). Thus God in His covenant is "the faithful God, keeping his covenant of love to a thousand generations of those who love him and keep his commands" (Deut. 7:9).

In contractual relationships the parties are responsible to each other for specific promises, but they are not personally vulnerable to each other. Covenant relationships require personal vulnerability and commitment.

God's covenant with the first family was more than a contract. It was a promise, freely given by God, of steadfast love toward His children. It called for total obedience and loyalty in return for His loving provision and care. It was a sovereign act of grace, calling for eternal commitment.

The purpose of God's covenant was to provide the security of a binding love within which the human family could live in harmony with Him and with one another.

The Tragedy of Adam's Fall

Adam and Eve were created in the image of God, fully capable of making and keeping commitments. But they failed to recognize that their ability to keep God's covenant was ultimately dependent upon their obedience to Him.

Blinded by Satan (who was himself the first covenant-breaker), Adam and Eve disobeyed. They made a contract with Satan and broke their covenant with God. As Saint Augustine perceived, they gave to the creature the love which belongs to the Creator alone. Because of their misguided love, the whole human family was cursed with brokenness.

In fewer than ten generations, "the Lord saw how great man's wickedness on the earth had become, and that every inclination of the thoughts of his heart was only evil all the time" (Gen. 6:5).

But despite continued rebellion on the part of His children, God cared enough for His family to renew His covenant with them. He lovingly opened up a new beginning for them through Noah: "But Noah found favor in the eyes of the Lord...Noah was a righteous man, blameless among the people of his time, and he walked with God" (Gen. 6:8,9).

To seal His covenant with Noah, God placed a rainbow in the sky, calling to remembrance His act of grace. "I establish my covenant with you: Never again will all life be cut off by the waters of a flood; never again will there be a flood to destroy the earth" (Gen. 9:11).

So God has continued to remain vulnerable to His children by renewing His covenant from generation to generation—through Abraham, Isaac, Jacob, Joseph, Moses, David and, ultimately, through Jesus Christ our Lord.

The apostle Paul recognized and reverenced this covenantal family bond that culminated in the death and resurrection of Jesus. In writing to the Ephesian church he exclaims, "For this reason I kneel before the Father, from whom his whole family in heaven and on earth derives its name'' (Eph. 3:14,15).

The Redemption of the Family

To establish the covenant of redemption, God personally came into the human family. In his letter to the Galatians Paul tells us that ''when the time had fully come, God sent His Son, born of a woman, born under law, to redeem those under law, that we might receive the full rights of sons. Because you are sons, God sent the Spirit of his Son into our hearts, the Spirit who calls out, 'Abba, Father.' So you are no longer a slave, but a son; and since you are a son, God has made you also an heir'' (Gal. 4:4-7).

Through Jesus, the covenant broken by the first Adam was restored. God was united with His family again. The apostle Paul explained this ultimate renewal of the covenant—and a promise of eternal life for the family of God—to the churches at Rome and Corinth:

> We also joy in God through our Lord Jesus Christ, by whom we have now received the atonement. Wherefore, as by one man sin entered into the world, and death by sin; and so death passed upon all men, for that all have sinned....Therefore as by the offense of one judgment came upon all men to condemnation; even so by the righteousness of one the free gift came upon all men unto justification of life. For as by one man's disobedience many were made sinners, so by the obedience of one shall many be made righteous (Rom. 5:11,12,18,19, KJV).

> For since by man came death, by man came also the resurrection of the dead. For as in Adam all die, even so in Christ shall all be made alive (1 Cor. 15:21,22, KJV).

Christ died to save all mankind. This includes families. Biblical historians remind us that in the early church people tended to be converted not just one at a time, as individuals, but as families. As Paul admonished the Philippian jailer, "Believe in the Lord Jesus, and you will be saved—you *and your household*" (Acts 16:31, emphasis added).

Concern for the salvation of families is also reflected in other passages:

> To the rest I say this (I, not the Lord): If any brother has a wife who is not a believer and she is willing to live with him, he must not divorce her. And if a woman has a husband who is not a believer and he is willing to live with her, she must not divorce him. For the unbelieving husband has been sanctified through his wife, and the unbelieving wife has been sanctified through her believing husband. Otherwise your children would be unclean, but as it is, they are holy (1 Cor. 7:12-14).

> Wives, in the same way be submissive to your husbands so that, if any of them do not believe the word, they may be won over without words by the behavior of their wives (1 Pet. 3:1).

The Church as Family

The gospel celebrated by early Christians called people out of sensual and materialistic Roman culture into God's spiritual and eternal family. In His discussion with Nicodemus, Jesus described entry into this family as a new birth:

"I tell you the truth, no one can see the kingdom of God unless he is born again."

"How can a man be born when he is old?" Nicodemus asked. "Surely he cannot enter a second time into his mother's womb to be born!"

Jesus answered, "I tell you the truth, no one can enter the kingdom of God unless he is born of water and the Spirit. Flesh gives birth to flesh, but the Spirit gives birth to spirit. You should not be surprised at my saying, 'You must be born again' " (John 3:3-7).

Entrance into God's family through the new birth is symbolized by the ordinance of water baptism. We publicly declare our Christian faith by being baptized in water. As Jesus proclaimed, "Whoever believes and is baptized will be saved, but whoever does not believe will be condemned" (Mark 16:16).

We continue to acknowledge our faith in Christ through the celebration of communion. Beginning with the Last Supper, communion became a unifying celebration of continued participation in the life of God's family—a symbol of covenant and commitment. Every week the early church commemorated the Last Supper in remembrance of their Lord. Paul wrote to the Corinthians:

> For I received from the Lord what I also passed on to you: The Lord Jesus, on the night he was betrayed, took bread, and when he had given thanks, he broke it and said, "This is my body, which is for you; do this in remembrance of me." In the same way, after supper he took the cup, saying, "This cup is the new covenant in my blood; do this, whenever you drink it, in remembrance of me." For whenever you eat this bread and drink this cup, you proclaim the Lord's death until he comes.
>
> Therefore, whoever eats the bread or drinks the cup of the Lord in an unworthy manner will be guilty of sinning against the body and blood of the Lord (1 Cor. 11:23-27).

By sharing the bread and the cup, members of God's family were able to identify with their Lord and with each other on a regular basis.

God's Family Heals and Helps

Jesus emphasized the importance of the practical expression of the church's ministry:

Then the King will say to those on his right, "Come, you who are blessed by my Father; take your inheritance, the kingdom prepared for you since the creation of the world. For I was hungry and you gave me something to eat, I was thirsty and you gave me something to drink, I was a stranger and you invited me in, I needed clothes and you clothed me, I was sick and you looked after me, I was in prison and you came to visit me.''

Then the righteous will answer him, ''Lord, when did we see you hungry and feed you, or thirsty and give you something to drink? When did we see you a stranger and invite you in, or needing clothes and clothe you? When did we see you sick or in prison and go to visit you?''

The King will reply, ''I tell you the truth, whatever you did for one of the least of these brothers of mine, you did for me'' (Matt. 25:34-40).

Understanding these clear instructions of their Lord, the members of the early church cared for one another. They understood that being born again didn't just refer to their readiness for heaven. It also meant extending family ties beyond blood relationships. After all, Jesus taught us to pray, ''Our Father,'' and He taught us to call each other brother and sister. As Matthew records:

> While Jesus was still talking to the crowd, his mother and brothers stood outside, wanting to speak to him. Someone told him, ''Your mother and brothers are standing outside, wanting to speak to you.''
>
> He replied to him, ''Who is my mother, and who are my brothers?'' Pointing to his disciples, he said, ''Here are my mother and my brothers. For whoever does the will of my Father in heaven is my brother and sister and mother'' (Matt. 12:46-50).

Why did Jesus use this family metaphor in teaching His followers how to care for each other? He obviously intended that the family be the pattern of love and care to be followed throughout the history of the church.

Individual Versus Family

Our modern society champions individual rights and praises individual achievement. For more than two decades we have been immersed in the spirit of the "me" generation. Such a climate fosters competition at the expense of cooperation, and the pursuit of riches and pleasure at the cost of relationships.

More than any other religious leader, Jesus values the individual. Nevertheless, He calls us into a community of sacrificial love. The greatest challenge of Christian living is the cost of discipleship. Jesus sets the challenge before us:

> Then he called the crowd to him along with his disciples and said: "If anyone would come after me, he must deny himself and take up his cross and follow me. For whoever wants to save his life will lose it, but whoever loses his life for me and for the gospel will save it. What good is it for a man to gain the whole world, yet forfeit his soul? Or what can a man give in exchange for his soul?" (Mark 8:34-37).

We *cannot* follow Jesus without caring for others. Just take a look at the Sermon on the Mount. It is replete with references to the spiritual characteristics of authentic Christian community. For example:

Blessed are the peacemakers, for they will be called sons of God.

In the same way, let your light shine before men, that they may see your good deeds and praise your Father in heaven.

So in everything, do to others what you would have them do to you, for this sums up the Law and the Prophets (Matt. 5:9,16; 7:12).

The New Testament Church Focused on the Family

Caring for their families was the primary concern of first-century Christians. In his letter to Timothy, Paul gives a vivid picture of the value the early church placed on strong family bonds:

> But if a widow has children or grandchildren, these should learn first of all to put their religion into practice by caring for their own family and so repaying their parents and grandparents, for this is pleasing to God. The widow who is really in need and left all alone puts her hope in God and continues night and day to pray and to ask God for help. But the widow who lives for pleasure is dead even while she lives. Give the people these instructions, too, so that no one may be open to blame. If anyone does not provide for his relatives, and especially for his immediate family, he has denied the faith and is worse than an unbeliever (1 Tim. 5:4-8).

James also emphasizes this concern:

What good is it, my brothers, if a man claims to have faith but has no deeds? Can such faith save him? Suppose a brother or sister is without clothes and daily food. If one of you says to him, "Go, I wish you well; keep warm and well fed," but does nothing about his physical needs, what good is it? In the same way, faith by itself, if it is not accompanied by action, is dead (James 2:14-17).

The first crisis in the New Testament church centered in family care. The apostles' zeal to convert the world began to overshadow caring for the practical needs of brothers and sisters. Christian widows and orphans were being neglected. How different is this from today? All too often the church prides itself on giving to evangelize the world, while at the same time largely ignoring its hurting members and failing to give assistance to the poor of its own communities.

However, in the first-century church, family complaints grew to the point where they got the attention of the elders. Out of necessity, they temporarily diverted their attention away from evangelism and toward pastoral care. Not until deacons were appointed to provide properly for the widows and orphans of the church were the apostles free to return to the task of world evangelism (see Acts 6:1-7).

The church today still hears the complaints of its people—stressed marriages; lonely singles; hurting divorcees; displaced children; delinquent teenagers; frustrated, unemployed, abandoned senior citizens. And once again, if the church is to follow her crucified and

34

risen Lord, she must take the time to meet the needs of the bruised and brokenhearted.

Members of One Body

Referring to the function of the church, Paul reminds us:

> The body is a unit, though it is made up of many parts; and though all its parts are many, they form one body. So it is with Christ. For we were all baptized by one Spirit into one body—whether Jews or Greeks, slave or free— and we were all given the one Spirit to drink.
>
> Now the body is not made up of one part but of many....But God has combined the members of the body and has given greater honor to the parts that lacked it, so that there should be no division in the body, but that its parts should have equal concern for each other. If one part suffers, every part suffers with it; if one part is honored, every part rejoices with it. Now you are the body of Christ, and each one of you is a part of it'' (1 Cor. 12:12-14,24-27).

In this beautiful metaphor the Holy Spirit directs the body of Christ to care for its members and reminds them of their covenantal relationship with each other. Paul follows this admonition with a description of the dynamic essential to Christian care: divine love. Without the energy of divine love, this kind of care is impossible.

In the following chapters we will offer specific suggestions for facilitating the expression of divine love through the ministries of the church. However, without this essential dynamic, organized programs—no matter how carefully engineered—will take on the appearance of just another well-intentioned fad.

Suggested Readings—Chapter Two

Jan and Myron Chartier, *Caring Together: Faith, Hope, and Love in Your Family* (Westminster Press, 1986).

Jim Larson, *Growing a Healthy Family* (Augsburg Publishing House, 1986).

Roy Matheson, *Loving God's Family* (Victor Books, 1985).

Royce Money, *Building Stronger Families* (Victor Books, 1984).

Elvin M. Powers, *Building a Caring-Sharing Community of Believers* (Beacon Hill, 1983).

George Rekers, *Family Building: Six Qualities of a Strong Family* (Regal, 1985).

Wayne Rickerson, *Strengthening the Family* (Standard Publishing, 1987).

Lindell Sawyers, *Faith and Families* (Westminster Press, 1986).

The Family-Friendly Pastor

M any churches measure a pastor's effectiveness by the number of people who attend Sunday services or by the response to sermons, or by the size of the offerings. If these are the criteria by which the minister is evaluated, then naturally he will design programs aimed at getting results in these areas.

But ask yourself: If a pastor were highly successful in these areas, would that alone make you want to be a member of his church? If not, what are the other important aspects of ministry you would hope to find?

Perhaps these other aspects of ministry could be identified by answering the following questions: If you were a stranger in your city, what criteria would you use in deciding which church to attend? Would your decision be based solely on the pastor's ability as a preacher? How highly would you rank the church's emphasis on family ministry? What role would your children's needs play in your choice? What would you look for to help you gauge the pastor's concern for your family?

Getting to Know Your Families

Kevin and Karen had been transferred. Kevin's company had offered him a promotion that required them to move more than a thousand miles from the area where they had raised their family. They soon found a church that they hoped would meet their spiritual needs and help them find new friends.

They were dedicated Christians and looked forward to being actively involved in their new church home. Indeed, only a few weeks had passed before their new pastor asked both Kevin and Karen to assume leadership responsibilities. Time passed. Four years later, even after a great deal of faithful service in their church, they still felt isolated and lonely—a feeling they had never experienced in their previous church life.

Most pastors would agree that there is a shortage of people like Kevin and Karen—regular attenders, willing workers, faithful tithers. Most pastors would be thrilled to have such people—already mature in faith and ready to go to work—move into their community. But having placed them in lay leadership, how many pastors would anticipate having to meet this family's needs for new friends and a new support system?

Kevin and Karen had teenagers and aging parents

living with them. No one from the church reached out to them. Even though they were disappointed with such an apparent lack of concern, they faithfully fulfilled their responsibilities. Being human, they did complain to each other once in a while, though they always felt vaguely guilty when they did.

Often we pastors are keenly aware of the lack of lay commitment to church ministries. We are too prone to complain about this, even from the pulpit. But how sensitive are we to our church's lack of commitment to the personal needs of our families—particularly to newcomers? Are we as committed to the families of our churches as we expect them to be to the church?

Many of us can quote our most recent attendance and offering figures. But can we cite the number of family units in our church? We are all too familiar with the recruiting needs we face. Are we as closely in touch with the unique needs of our families?

The statistics by which we measure church growth are better suited to tracing the profit and loss of a business than to assessing the adequacy of pastoral care for families. They speak of contracts rather than covenants. A truly pastoral model requires a different kind of analysis.

Perhaps answering the following questions will be more helpful in determining family needs (the list is by no means exhaustive):

• How many families in your church have recently moved into your community from out of town?

• During the past year, how many of your wage earners have been without jobs?

• How many of your family units are headed by single people?

• How many of your senior citizens live alone—at a distance from their children?

• How many of your people are handicapped?

• How many of your couples have recently divorced?

• In the past year, how many unwanted pregnancies have there been? How many juvenile arrests? How many battered wives? How many molested or abused children?

Most people who come to church have needs and are anxious to have them met. People seldom forget the pastor who remembers their needs.

For pastors who want to minister to such practical family needs, this information is not difficult to obtain. To assist you in obtaining it, you might try distributing a family needs assessment card like the one shown on page 41. Notice that the card can be completed anonymously if desired. This enables those who want personal attention to receive it and, at the same time, permits those who want to remain anonymous to contribute information that will be useful to the pastor.

Sharing the Pastoral Burden

Becoming keenly aware of family needs can be overwhelming. But don't get discouraged. You have a wide range of resources at your disposal in the staff, the board and the departmental ministries of the church. These resources should be viewed and utilized as extensions of the pastor's care for the family of God.

The pastor must teach those he recruits that Christian leaders are servants. Our position is one of service,

Family Needs Assessment Card

Check appropriate spaces below:

Personal status: ____ Married ____ Single ____ Separated

____ Divorced ____ Remarried

Age:

____ Under 18 ____ 18-24 ____ 25-29 ____ 30s ____ 40s

____ 50s ____ 60s ____ 70s ____ 80s ____ 90s

Number of children: ____ Ages of children: _____

Other relatives in the home: ____ Ages: _____

Special needs in your home:

____ Unemployment ____ Handicapped ____ Severe illness

____ Substance abuse

Other: _____

How long have you lived in the area? _____

_____

Optional

Name: _____

Address: _____

Phone: _____ Member: _____ Visitor: _____

I would like a pastoral visit: ____ Yes ____ No

I want to get involved in church ministry: ____ Yes ____ No

I would like to get involved in a care group: ____ Yes ____ No not status. We are to show the family of God how to care for each other. The towel and the basin are the symbols of our ministry.

Of course, the most effective method of teaching is modeling. If we want God's people to serve one another in love, then we must set the example.

Training Families to Care for Each Other

In a small church there is no janitor, no secretary, no assistant or associate. The pastor is the staff!

By the same token, however, the family units are also few in number. This gives you the opportunity to learn firsthand how to care for families in need. This is invaluable experience. After all, you can't teach what you haven't learned.

As your church grows you can train families to care for each other. This is how the early church did it. "Carry each other's burdens, and in this way you will fulfill the law of Christ" (Gal. 6:2).

Here are a few simple suggestions for helping families learn to care for each other:

• Include newcomers in after-church get-togethers.

• Carry in meals for families during crises created by illness or death.

• Provide lawn care for disabled or elderly people.

• Create an emergency fund for limited financial assistance to members in crisis.

• Offer occasional child care for single parents.

• Send cards on special occasions.

• Telephone or visit those who are shut in.

Inspiring members to provide such active love for one

The Family-Friendly Pastor

another will bring invaluable credibility to the witness of your church. You may not become known as the community's greatest pulpiteer. But you will be appreciated as a pastor who cares for his people.

When the people of your church are trained to care for others (both inside and outside the church), your church will grow. This was the secret of success in the early church:

> Every day they continued to meet together in the temple courts. They broke bread in their homes and ate together with glad and sincere hearts, praising God and enjoying the favor of all the people. And the Lord added to their number daily those who were being saved (Acts 2:46-47).

Office Equipment Can Help

Obtaining information about members, visitors and regular attenders can help people care for each other. A personal computer can be invaluable to the pastor in this task. By properly storing pertinent information about each family or individual, the pastor can make his telephone conversations and personal visits more meaningful.

For example, if you are talking on the telephone, you can retrieve the person's family data on the screen and refer to it in your conversation. Or, if you are making personal visits, you can print it out before you leave and take it with you.

Although answering machines lack a certain personal touch, until your church can afford a secretary they can track incoming calls for you, both in the office and at the parsonage. In fact, a creative message on the answering device can leave people with a positive feeling about you and the church.

Training Your Board to Serve

Lay people selected to serve on the board of the church often are given very little training in caring for others. This has emphatically been the case in most of the horror stories that I have heard about pastor-board conflicts. If the people who are chosen to serve on the board of their church are unfamiliar with what this involves, they can easily come to see their task as that of sitting on the board of a labor union or a secular corporation. Such a mind-set seeks status rather than service. The result is that board members may think their role is to tell the pastor what to do rather than to help the pastor care for the family of God.

The wise pastor will provide a special time of training for board members. This can take the convenient format of a Saturday seminar. The curriculum should include an emphasis on the biblical basis of the church board, the theology of lay leadership, a review of denominational history, a review of the constitution and by-laws of the local congregation, and a description of specific duties and portfolios to be assigned board members. The pastor should teach the more critical subjects, but experienced board members may also be given an opportunity to teach some of the sessions.

An informal lunch with the board on this occasion can help build a healthy rapport for the year of service ahead. Such a practice is grounded in biblical tradition and will help to build a sense of family among leaders of the church.

Our God does not build walls between His children; He spreads tables for them. The Bible is full of examples: the Passover and other Old Testament feasts, the Last Supper and the marriage supper of the Lamb, to mention only a few. As Isaiah reminds us, God calls His children to feast with Him as a means of renewing their covenant with Him and with each other (see Is. 55:1-5).

Jesus used occasions of eating for building relationships with His disciples and others. Don't overlook the potential of this ministry in creating a sense of community within your church family. The annual church picnic, a potluck supper before the annual business meeting, an annual reception for new members—all give opportunities for families to become acquainted with one another and with the leadership of the church.

These times together relax people's defenses and foster an awareness of family needs that might otherwise go unnoticed. While eating and sharing together, people are naturally motivated to become more vulnerable to each other and to care for one another.

Adding Staff Members

The richest resource of any congregation is its people. Before assuming the cost of additional paid staff, recruit volunteer help from the church family. Committed and competent volunteer part-time secretarial and janitorial workers can often be found in the congregation. As the church grows you may also find part-time volunteer lay staff to help with music, Christian education, youth and other departmental ministries.

A capable secretary should probably be the first addition to your full-time staff. This person can help organize and coordinate the work of the church office, which is essential to maximizing the productivity of lay volunteers. It also paves the way for other full-time staff members to be added later.

The order in which additional staff members are called should be determined by the needs of the community and your particular church. For example, if you are ministering in the retirement community and most of your members are over fifty years of age, you would probably want to consider adding a full-time minister of pastoral care before you add a minister of music. On the other hand, if you are in a rapidly growing community, the possibilities of adding a minister of evangelism or minister of youth might be uppermost on your mind.

Whatever the office, care should be taken to see that those called are capable of the tasks for which they are chosen. Sometimes we make the mistake of choosing people on the basis of friendship rather than competence. This can be disastrous to friendship and to the effectiveness of the ministerial team.

For example, many parsonage couples meet at conventions and have a great time together in after-service socializing. They may assume mistakenly that the fun and energy generated in their social times can be automatically transferred into productive ministry together.

Certainly you want people on staff who are socially compatible. But don't put the cart before the horse. First of all, make sure that new staff members possess the character, gifts and talents necessary to get the job done. Then you can worry about social compatibility. In other words, social compatibility is a necessary, but not sufficient, sign of God's will in your choice of staff personnel. The critical factor is their ability to be effective in the position for which they are chosen.

Caring for the Staff

No doubt there will be philosophical differences among pastors as to how their own families will be cared for. Some pastors may feel free to share their own needs with members of the staff, while others may choose to build a support group among other ministers outside their congregation. However, the care of staff families is the responsibility of the pastor.

This may be done through times of prayer at regular staff meetings, on staff retreats, and at other times of fellowship. By lovingly caring for the staff, the pastor models the relationship he wants them to have with those under their care.

Only when the leaders of the church are nurtured and spiritually healthy are they able to provide the strength and direction necessary for meaningful corporate worship. As Paul reminded the church at Ephesus,

> So He has given some to be apostles and others
> to be prophets; some to be evangelists and others
> to be pastors and teachers, to equip the saints

for the task of ministering toward the building up of the body of Christ, until we all may arrive at the unity of faith and that understanding of that Son of God that brings completeness of personality, tending toward the measure of the stature of the fullness of Christ.

Telling the truth in love, we should grow up in every way toward Him who is the Head— Christ, from whom the entire body is fitted together and united by every contributing ligament, with proportionate power for each single part to effect the development of the body for its upbuilding in love (Eph. 4:11-13,15,16, NBV).

Suggested Readings—Chapter Three

Garth Bolinder, John R. Cionca and Tom McKee, *What Every Pastor Needs to Know about Music, Youth and Education* (*Christianity Today*, 1986).

Robert Thornton Henderson, *Beating the Churchgoing Blahs* (InterVarsity Press, 1986).

Frank H. Olsen, *Church Staff Support: Cultivating & Maintaining Staff Relationships* (Augsburg, 1982).

Wayne Paulson, *Parish Secretary's Handbook* (Augsburg, 1983).

Richard B. Sargent and John E. Benson, *Computers in the Church: Practical Assistance in Making the*

Computer Decision (Augsburg, 1986).

Melvin J. Steinbron, *Can the Pastor Do It Alone?* (Regal, 1987).

Cynthia Thero, *Can I Help? A Practical Guide to the Care and Feeding of Volunteers* (Tabor, 1987).

Edgar Walz, *How to Manage Your Church: A Manual for Pastors and Lay Leaders* (Concordia, 1986).

Thomas F. Zimmerman, Zenas J. Bicket and G. Raymond Carlson, *And He Gave Pastors* (Gospel Publishing, 1978).

Family-Friendly Worship

Just as a father longs for loving communion with his children, so God seeks the worship of His family. In His conversation with the woman of Samaria, Jesus movingly illustrates the importance of worship by reminding us that

> a time is coming and has now come when the true worshipers will worship the Father in spirit and truth, for they are the kind of worshipers the Father seeks. God is spirit, and his worshipers must worship in spirit and in truth (John 4:23,24).

The woman, seeking to avoid her spiritual need, tried to engage Jesus in debate over the proper place for worship. But far more important than the *place* of worship is the *spirit* of worship—an acknowledgment of our spiritual hunger and thirst. This is why Jesus avoided the woman's challenge to a superficial theological debate and insisted on confronting her with her own spiritual thirst.

One of the greatest challenges facing the pastor today is to lead God's people in authentic worship, helping them express their spiritual need and accept God's gift of grace. Our tendency is to deny our ultimate dependence on God and each other. We pretend to be self-sufficient. But by encouraging an atmosphere of spiritual transparency and brokenness in worship, the pastor can provide God's family an opportunity for forgiveness, renewal and community.

In the story of the Pharisee and the publican, Jesus illustrates the stark contrast between authentic worship and just "playing church." The Pharisee went to the synagogue merely to be seen by men. He wanted to be known as a God-fearing churchgoer, but he blatantly denied his spiritual need. Listen to his prayer:

> The Pharisee stood up and prayed about himself: "God, I thank you that I am not like all other men—robbers, evildoers, adulterers—or even like this tax collector. I fast twice a week and give a tenth of all I get" (Luke 18:11,12).

On the other hand, the publican attending the same service honestly acknowledged his sin and openly cried out to God for help. Listen to his prayer: "God, have mercy on me, a sinner" (Luke 18:13). What transparency!

What vulnerability!

Jesus wanted His disciples to know the difference between a churchgoer and a worshipper. This parable vividly reveals the spirit of authentic worship—worship that results in personal change. The Pharisee went to church. The publican *worshipped*. The Pharisee prayed within himself, denying his own spiritual need. The publican openly confessed his sin to God. The Pharisee went home the same man he was when he came. The publican went home a new man—relieved of his sins and changed by God's grace.

Through the story of Jesus' conversation with the woman of Samaria and the parable of the Pharisee and the publican, the Bible emphasizes the importance of teaching people how to worship in spirit and in truth. Often we make the mistake of assuming that if people know how to go through the motions of worship, they know the true meaning of worship. Nothing could be further from the truth.

Teaching the Purpose of Worship

Recognition of our family relationship with God is evidenced by a desire to gather with other members of God's family to worship Him. Our attendance at worship service symbolizes our gratitude and commitment to God. We are grateful to Him for His love and grace. We are committed to offering Him our lives as channels of His love and grace to others.

Paul gives Roman Christians the following instruction in worship:

> Therefore, I urge you, brothers, in view of God's mercy, to offer your bodies as living sacrifices, holy and pleasing to God—this is your spiritual act of worship (Rom. 12:1).

This is what worship is all about—a regular, communal expression of spiritual commitment.

Worship encourages a spirit of renewal—renewal of our commitment to God, the renewal of our commitment to each other. At the same time, it reminds us of a spiritual void in our lives that only Christ can fill. Remember the words of Jesus: "It is not the healthy who need a doctor, but the sick" (Matt. 9:12).

The pastor should not assume that all members of God's family come to the worship service prepared to worship. He knows that more often than not, people come into the sanctuary preoccupied with personal struggles and crowded schedules. Accepting this reality, he is ready to help God's people prepare their hearts for authentic worship. Either through an embellished liturgical call to worship or an effective extemporaneous one, the pastor, by revealing his own desire for spiritual renewal, will lead his people in a meaningful worship experience.

For example, at an appropriate time early in the service the pastor may say something like this:

> I don't know what moved you to be in God's house today. But I've come to worship God because I need His grace. Only as each of us is sensitive to his or her own personal needs will this service be what God wants it to be—an

exchange of our weakness for His strength. God says to you and me, "My grace is sufficient for you, for My strength is made perfect in weakness." Let us humble ourselves before the Lord in prayer and ask His blessing on our worship.

Preparing yourself for this fresh and transparent approach to worship may not be easy, but it yields rich rewards in the lives of people. Such openness on the part of the pastor at the beginning of each worship experience reminds people why they are in church and challenges them to discover and experience the meaning of authentic worship.

Teaching the Importance of Regular Worship

Just as children must be taught habits necessary for good physical health, so new Christians must learn some spiritual habits vital to good spiritual health. Staying physically healthy requires that we reserve special times and places for meeting the body's needs for nourishment and rest. In the same way, if people are to stay spiritually healthy they must learn to set aside special times and places for worship.

The Bible is replete with basic principles of corporate worship. The last half of the book of Exodus and the entire book of Deuteronomy are devoted to instructing Israel about places, times and special rules regarding worship. The first, second and fourth commandments underscore the vital role worship plays in the life of the child of God (see Ex. 20:3-17 and Deut. 5:7-21). Indeed, this basic lesson in spiritual discipline—the importance of setting aside special times and places for worship—is stressed throughout Scripture.

For example, we are told that God communed with Adam and Eve in the garden during the "cool of the day" (Gen. 3:8). The patriarchs were famous for their altars. God gave Moses specific plans for the construction of the tabernacle—Israel's place of worship after their flight from Egypt. During their nomadic life in the wilderness, the children of Israel regularly engaged in the covenant renewal ceremony, commemorating God's act of grace in delivering them from bondage in Egypt. Once they were established in their own land, Solomon's temple became the center of Israel's spiritual life.

Jesus recognized the importance of times and places for worship in His own life and ministry. For example, Luke tells us that Jesus was accustomed to attending the synagogue on the Sabbath.

> He went to Nazareth, where He had been brought up, and on the Sabbath day He went into the synagogue, as was His custom. And He stood up to read (Luke 4:16).

Luke also indicates that Peter and John had a habit of praying in the temple about the same time every day.

> One day Peter and John were going up to the temple at the time of prayer—at three in the afternoon (Acts 3:1).

Paul makes reference to the believers gathering regularly on the first day of the week:

> On the first day of every week, each one of you should set aside a sum of money in keeping with his income, saving it up, so that when I come no collections will have to be made (1 Cor. 16:2).

And the writer of the letter to the Hebrews admonishes us not to forsake the assembling of ourselves together for worship.

> Let us not give up meeting together, as some are in the habit of doing, but let us encourage one another—and all the more as you see the Day approaching (Heb. 10:25).

Teaching People to Respect Their Place of Worship

Each of us has the capacity to ascribe unique meaning to places and objects. Our government takes advantage of this in nourishing our patriotism through symbols, monuments and memorials. When we visit places like the White House and the Capitol rotunda we are awed by respect for these historic seats of government.

Regardless of how plain or ornate your church may be, the room set aside for worship is referred to as a sanctuary—a place of refuge or protection. Just as people learn appropriate behaviors for expressing patriotism and respect for national monuments, they need to be taught ways of expressing reverence for the sanctuary of God's house. Adults need to recognize the importance of modeling this reverence for their children.

This may be done by attaching a sense of awe and

wonder to our central place of worship. This respect for the sanctuary can be enhanced through an understanding of its architecture and furnishings.

If your chancel is divided, don't take it for granted that your people understand the difference between the function of the lectern and that of the pulpit. Remind your people that the pulpit speaks of the ability of God's Word to stand on its own—no man is needed to uphold it. In fact, it is the Book on the pulpit that gives importance to the man behind the pulpit.

When speaking from the pulpit, the man of God should seek to come to the people of God through the Word of God. The pulpit is no place for the expression of personal opinion. Preserving the pulpit for the preaching of God's sacred Word gives the Scripture a special place in your worship.

In churches with a divided chancel, the main focus of worship is on the Eucharist, when the priest or pastor celebrates communion. Share with your people the symbolism of the Old Testament tabernacle and the relationship between the outer court, the holy place and the holy of holies. This will give them a deeper appreciation for the increasing sacredness of the space between the prayer railing on either side of the front of the chancel and the altar at the rear. In this arrangement, the pastor's celebration of communion symbolizes the most holy expression of God's love—Christ offering Himself for the sins of the people (see Heb. 9:24-28).

Churches with an undivided chancel position the pulpit in the center and consider the preaching and teaching of the Word of God to be the central element of worship.

In this arrangement, the communion table stands on the floor of the sanctuary, symbolizing Christ among the people. The prayer railing or bench in front of the communion table speaks of our Lord's invitation to come boldly to the throne of grace, realizing that the sacrifice of Christ fully satisfies the righteous demands of a holy God. Between the person kneeling at the prayer railing and the Word of God supported by the pulpit stands the memory of Christ's broken body and shed blood, given to atone for our sin, reconciling us to God.

Teaching People to Participate in Worship

Corporate worship allows the family of God to benefit from a unique intensification of God-awareness through praise, song and prayer. The degree of participation on the part of the people will depend largely on the worship leader.

Praise

Praise opens the soul to God. David encourages us to "enter His gates with thanksgiving and His courts with praise; give thanks to Him and praise His name" (Ps. 100:4). Regardless of your worship style, concert praise intensifies the worship experience.

In more liturgical churches, people can be encouraged to read their praise expressively, with feeling. Many inspirational passages in the book of Psalms lend themselves to this kind of choral reading—especially Psalms 106, 111-113 and 146-150. These psalms all begin with "Praise the Lord."

Pastors whose churches are less formal and more

spontaneous in their style of worship can lead their people through other expressions of concert praise. Sometimes this may take the form of worship choruses. At other times people may be given an opportunity to express their praise and prayer in concert. And there are occasions when silent praise is very meaningful.

Song

Nothing accents a worship service like well-chosen and well-planned music. Music sets the tone. Musical themes can accent and embellish the sermon or they can diminish and detract from it.

I remember being in a Sunday morning worship service where I heard a Southern gospel song by the choir, gospel rock by a special ensemble and a Western gospel solo. Each musical expression led the people in a different direction. The music certainly did not prepare me to benefit from the pastor's message. In fact, I left the service confused, wondering what central message the pastor had in mind for the morning. Perhaps there was none.

On the other hand, when instrumental and vocal music is thematically planned around the pastor's message, the congregation is prepared to receive God's Word with a freshness of spirit that only music can inspire. Paul reminds us of the relationship between music and being filled with the Spirit.

> Do not get drunk on wine, which leads to debauchery. Instead, be filled with the Spirit. Speak to one another with psalms, hymns and spiritual songs. Sing and make music in your

heart to the Lord, always giving thanks to God the Father for everything, in the name of our Lord Jesus Christ (Eph. 5:18-20).

Prayer

Praise opens the soul to God, music sets the tone for the worship service, and prayer provides an opportunity to talk with God. Although different churches will ascribe different roles to prayer, most will include an invocation, a pastoral prayer and a benediction.

Whether written or extemporaneous, the purpose of the invocation is to acknowledge our need for God's forgiveness and blessing. Sometimes this is preceded by a call to prayer, which serves to draw the attention of the congregation away from the cares of the day to focus on the presence of God.

In the pastoral prayer, personal, family and other needs of the people are brought before God. Many churches mention specific needs presented through prayer requests. Prayer for local, state, national and world concerns can be offered at this time, along with prayers for denominational and church leaders. Some pastors pray for a different local congregation and its pastor each week. This helps lay people identify with the total Christian community and encourages a spirit of cooperation rather than competition among the family of God.

The pastoral prayer is the most important prayer of the day. It enables the pastor to identify with the needs of individuals and families in the congregation.

More churches are finding the pastoral prayer to be an excellent opportunity for ministering to one another—

anointing the sick with oil and praying for those with other personal needs. People are encouraged to extend the boundaries of family ties by reaching out in love to those around them. Some churches form small prayer circles of three or four people who pray for each other's needs. This is an excellent way to help people overcome spiritual shyness and extend themselves to others.

An inspiring benediction sends people out with a smile on their faces and a song in their hearts. They have been reminded that they are part of God's family—a family that extends beyond the bounds of time and space. They are not alone!

The Sermon

We preachers tend to be so preoccupied with the content and delivery of our sermons that we fail to notice what the people actually hear us say. This was delightfully illustrated in a cartoon I saw years ago. A hopeless-looking woman was leaving church. As the pastor reached out to shake her hand, she said, "Thank you, pastor, for your sermon this morning. It was just like water to a drowning man."

Too often, ministers choose to preach to their own needs or from their latest interests. This may be the result of poor planning. By planning your pulpit work at least six months in advance, you can have greater confidence that you are addressing the needs of your congregation. Through the wise use of needs-assessment surveys and prayerful reflection on the information they provide, the pastor can direct his preaching to the specific needs of his congregation.

One of the most effective ways to improve the worship experience for your people is to put yourself in their place and listen to a tape recording of your sermons once in a while. Then ask yourself:

• What is the prevailing emotional tone in my voice? Is it tense, angry, high-strung?

• Is there a sense of compassion as well as conviction in the delivery?

• Of what practical help would this message be to me?

• What biblical truth was explicated?

• What useful information was conveyed?

• Was it too long?

Early in my ministry I started asking myself questions like these. I wondered, What am I really telling my congregation about *me* when I preach? These kinds of questions prompted me to devote my doctoral dissertation to defining the function of the sermon in the pastor's role as counselor. One of the most important things I discovered in my study was that the pastor, either knowingly or unknowingly, does indeed reveal a great deal about himself through his sermons.

I was also curious to learn if the way a person presented himself in a sermon would have any effect on the number of people who later sought his counsel. To research this question I devised the sermon-content preference scale. This consisted of nine pairs of sermon paragraphs, three pairs devoted to each of three commonly held evangelical beliefs. Pastors surveyed were asked to choose the paragraph in each pair that most nearly represented the way they would prefer to express themselves. A panel of judges rated the paragraphs on three bipolar scales: nurturant versus threatening, person-centered versus dogma-centered, and this-worldly versus other-worldly.

The pastors involved in the study were also asked to give the amount of time they spent in counseling each week and the number of people they saw. The study revealed that, regardless of the area of doctrinal belief involved in the sermon, pastors who expressed themselves from the pulpit in more nurturant, person-centered and this-worldly terms were more often sought as counselors than pastors whose sermons came through in threatening, dogma-centered and other-worldly terms.

Preaching and Teaching

Jesus stressed the importance of both preaching and teaching in establishing His kingdom. Preaching confronts the unbeliever with his sin and challenges him to be reconciled to God by accepting Christ as Savior. Teaching confronts the believer with the need to accept responsibility for applying Christ's message to daily relationships, recognizing Jesus as Lord.

The need for balance in these ministries is seen in the two versions of the Great Commission presented by Mark and Matthew. Mark's version of the Great Commission emphasizes the importance of *preaching* the gospel of Jesus Christ to the whole world. Matthew's version of the Great Commission stresses the importance of *teaching* believers how to apply the gospel in their daily lives.

The pastor is challenged to be both a preacher and a teacher. Few pastors do both equally well. The selection of staff personnel and visiting speakers can complement the particular gifts of the pastor.

The sermon may serve either the preaching or teaching purpose. But doing both is difficult. In preparing his sermon, the pastor will want to determine the primary focus of his message.

A preaching sermon is aimed at bringing the hearer to a decision that results in a spiritual experience. A teaching sermon shows the hearer how to translate his spiritual experience into a Christ-centered life. Preaching confronts the hearer with what ought to be done. Teaching explains how to do it. We need how-tos to go with our ought-tos.

Of course, the most effective teaching sermon is the life of the minister himself. Modeling is the most powerful form of teaching. Remember, Jesus molded the lives of twelve men who would change the world by His two-word challenge, "Follow Me."

Suggested Readings—Chapter Four

Ronald Barclay Allen and Gordon Borror, *Worship: Rediscovering the Mission Jewel* (Multnomah, 1987).

Robert Berglund, *A Philosophy of Church Music* (Moody, 1985).

Calvin M. Johansson, *Music & Ministry: A Biblical Counterpoint* (Hendrickson, Mass., 1984).

Graham Kendrick, *Learning to Worship as a Way of Life* (Bethany House, 1985).

Cecil B. Knight, *Pentecostal Worship* (Pathway Press, 1974).

Ralph P. Martin, *The Worship of God: Some Theological, Pastoral & Practical Reflections* (Eerdmans, 1982).

Paul L. Walker, *The Ministry of Worship* (Pathway Press, 1981).

Edward K. Ziegler, *Prayers for Public Worship* (Brethren, 1986).

Family-Friendly Ordinances

We are reminded of our covenantal relationship with our heavenly Father and with each other every time we observe the ordinances of the church. In *Systematic Theology* (Judson Press) A.H. Strong notes that ordinances are "those outward rites which Christ has appointed to be administered in His church as visible signs of the saving truth of the gospel."

Most Protestants recognize two ordinances: baptism and communion. Although the church emphasizes their theological significance, we will focus on what might be called the therapeutic benefits of baptism and communion.

Since baptism and communion are repetitive functions

in the life of the church, they can easily become routine, their meaning diminished for both pastor and parishioner. If repetitive functions are to achieve any practical purpose they must be imbued with meaning. Baptism and communion pose this challenge for the pastor—he must make them meaningful for his parishioners.

Baptism

Jesus commands His disciples to baptize those who believe His gospel (see Matt. 28:19; Mark 16:16). Baptism symbolizes the death and burial of the old Adamic life and the birth and celebration of new life in Christ. Baptism publicly symbolizes our birth into the family of God.

Some argue that water baptism is not essential for the believer, citing the pardon of the thief on the cross as proof. But a clear reading of the New Testament shows that the thief on the cross was an exception that underscores, not lessens, the rule of baptism for believers. Christ's death atones for our sins; baptism is the public act that testifies to the church and community that we have accepted Him as our Lord.

The church has never seen baptism as optional. Jesus commanded it, and the apostles strictly obeyed. The high priority placed on baptism in the theology of the apostles is clearly seen in the way the subject is treated in the Acts of the Apostles: whenever baptism was physically possible, it was required.

At Jerusalem on the day of Pentecost, Peter's invitation was:

> Repent and be baptized, every one of you, in the name of Jesus Christ for the forgiveness of your sins. And you will receive the gift of the Holy Spirit (Acts 2:38).

The Ethiopian eunuch Philip led to the Lord was so anxious to be baptized that he said, "Look, here is water. Why shouldn't I be baptized?" (Acts 8:36).

The miraculous healing and baptism of Saul of Tarsus is recorded faithfully:

> Then Ananias went to the house and entered it. Placing his hands on Saul, he said, "Brother Saul, the Lord—Jesus, who appeared to you on the road as you were coming here—has sent me so that you may see again and be filled with the Holy Spirit." Immediately, something like scales fell from Saul's eyes, and he could see again. He got up and was baptized (Acts 9:17-18).

After the Gentiles at Cornelius's house accepted Christ as Savior and were filled with the Holy Spirit, Peter "ordered that they be baptized in the name of Jesus Christ" (Acts 10:48).

Paul said to the Ephesian believers:

> "John's baptism was a baptism of repentance. He told the people to believe in the One coming after him, that is, in Jesus." On hearing this they were baptized into the name of the Lord Jesus (Acts 19:4-5).

The Baptismal Service

The ordinance of baptism publicly introduces the believer to his new family in Christ. Therefore, the baptismal service should be one of the high points in the life of the church. The baptismal service is not just for the new believer. It is a community experience. It is a time for celebration, a time for reflection, a time for recommitment.

Celebration

In celebrating the new believer's entry into the spiritual family of the church, opportunity should be given for testimony. Hearing a sincere experience of the baptismal candidates' appreciation for God's saving grace can stimulate a fresh response in the hearts of the entire congregation.

Reflection

Baptism invites reflection. During the baptismal service, encourage those who are witnessing the event to relive their own rebirth and to reflect on the difference Christ has made in their lives. You also may want to confront them with the need to acknowledge certain aspects of self that still must be nailed to Christ's cross and buried with Him. You may want to challenge your people to see ways in which their lives can be made more and more reflective of Christ's life.

Recommitment

By experiencing the enthusiasm and sincerity of new believers, all believers can be challenged to recommit their lives to Christ and to each other. A strong plea can be made for those who are older in their faith to model for these new believers an unselfish life of love and service to God, their brothers and sisters in Christ, and their community.

Infant Baptism and Baby Dedication

Both infant baptism and baby dedication celebrate the grace of God in bringing a new life into His family. Although the primary responsibility for that life belongs to the parents, on this occasion the entire church community should be reminded of its role in nurturing the life and faith of the child.

Challenge the adult members of the congregation to model healthy Christian character before the child. Their love and prayers for the child should also be solicited. Not all service manuals provide for this emphasis so you may have to improvise a service of your own.

You may also want to help parishioners reflect on the symbolism of the baptistry or baptismal font and on the difference Christ has made in their lives each time they come to church. This might be done by several means:

• Put an explanation of the symbolism of the sanctuary in the bulletin.

• Direct special lighting onto the baptistry before the service formally begins.

• Focus hymns or gospel songs on the subject of baptism.

These are just a few ways of bringing people's attention to this important dimension of their faith.

Communion

The first communion service was instituted by Jesus after He had celebrated the feast of Passover with His disciples. Here is Matthew's account:

> While they were eating, Jesus took bread, gave thanks and broke it, and gave it to his disciples, saying, "Take and eat; this is my body."
> Then he took the cup, gave thanks and offered it to them, saying, "Drink from it, all of you. This is my blood of the covenant, which is poured out for many for the forgiveness of sins. I tell you, I will not drink of this fruit of the vine from now on until that day when I drink it anew with you in my Father's kingdom" (Matt. 26:26-29).

The church came to view this celebration of our Lord with His disciples as distinct from the Jewish feast of Passover and commonly referred to it as the Last Supper. In commemoration of the Last Supper, the early church regularly held an *agape* meal in conjunction with the celebration of communion. In his letter to the Corinthians, Paul addressed some abuses and excesses associated with this practice:

> In the following directives I have no praise for you, for your meetings do more harm than good. In the first place, I hear that when you come together as a church, there are divisions among you, and to some extent I believe it. No doubt there have to be differences among you to show

72

which of you have God's approval. When you come together, it is not the Lord's Supper you eat, for as you eat, each of you goes ahead without waiting for anybody else. One remains hungry, another gets drunk. Don't you have homes to eat and drink in? Or do you despise the church of God and humiliate those who have nothing? What shall I say to you? Shall I praise you for this? Certainly not!

For I received from the Lord what I also passed on to you: The Lord Jesus, on the night He was betrayed, took bread, and when He had given thanks, He broke it and said, "This is My body, which is for you; do this in remembrance of Me." In the same way, after supper He took the cup, saying, "This cup is the new covenant in My blood; do this, whenever you drink it, in remembrance of me." For whenever you eat this bread and drink this cup, you proclaim the Lord's death until He comes.

Therefore, whoever eats the bread or drinks the cup of the Lord in an unworthy manner will be guilty of sinning against the body and blood of the Lord. A man ought to examine himself before he eats of the bread and drinks of the cup. For anyone who eats and drinks without recognizing the body of the Lord eats and drinks judgment on himself. That is why many among you are weak and sick, and a number of you have fallen asleep. But if we judged ourselves, we would not come under judgment. When we are judged by the Lord, we are being disciplined so that we will not be condemned with the world.

So then, my brothers, when you come together to eat, wait for each other. If anyone is hungry, he should eat at home, so that when you meet together it may not result in judgment (1 Cor. 11:17-34).

Giving Thanks

The earliest name given communion by the church is Eucharist, derived from *eucharistia* ("giving of thanks"). Later in the history of the church, the *agape* meal diminished in importance and the Eucharist (the blessing of the bread and the cup) became more prominent. Today, for many Christians, the Eucharist alone is known as the Lord's Supper. However, there are still some groups that recognize the historic difference and, on occasion, celebrate the *agape* meal along with communion and the pedolavium (footwashing). Whenever this is done, the meal and accompanying footwashing should be structured so that maximum opportunity is given for exchange of forgiveness and reaffirmation of loving unity among members of the body of Christ.

Among Protestants there are three basic doctrinal views of the physical elements involved in communion. The oldest is consubstantiation, the view held by Luther. Although he rejected the "miracle" of the Roman Catholic mass, whereby the elements of communion are believed to be transformed into the literal body and blood of Christ (transubstantiation), Luther insisted that the literal body of Christ is present with the bread and cup of communion.

A generation after Luther, John Calvin rejected Luther's view of communion as being too close to the Catholic doctrine. He taught that the bread and cup were signs of the true spiritual communication Christians have through the body and blood of our Lord.

Calvin's predecessor, Ulrich Zwingli, also rejected both the Catholic and the Lutheran positions. He believed that the doctrine of transubstantiation encouraged the superstition that material means could be used to secure spiritual blessing. For Zwingli, Luther's position was still not far enough removed from transubstantiation to secure the doctrine of justification by faith through grace alone. Therefore, he insisted that communion is a celebration of thanksgiving in memory of Christ's death. The bread and cup are symbols of Christ's body and blood, given as signs of an eternal covenant between God and His children.

Regardless of your theology, the communion service has great potential for the healing of God's family. In communion we share together the memory and the meaning of the broken body and shed blood of Christ.

Memory and Meaning

How does the pastor make this memory and meaning real to the family of God?

First, when communion is celebrated it should be the center of the worship service. Song and praise should focus on the communion theme. In honor of the communion service, the sermon should be brief, supporting the spiritual import of communion—the miracle and memory of Calvary.

Second, the elements must have real meaning for the pastor before he can make their meaning real to others. The bread must be more than just bread. The cup must be more than just the fruit of the vine. In his own way, the pastor must help his flock discern in these symbols the body and blood of the Lord.

Care should be taken not to rush through the distribution and partaking of the elements. Ask God to make you especially sensitive to the spiritual needs of those present. Give the people plenty of time for spiritual reflection and self-examination.

During the partaking of the bread, lead the people in expressing gratitude for health and faith for healing. Help them reflect on the purpose of Christ's sufferings. Here is an example of the kind of prayer I would consider helpful to people seeking personal meaning in partaking of the bread:

> Father, as we hold this broken bread in our hands, remind us of the broken body of Your Son. He was wounded for our transgressions. He was bruised for our iniquities. The chastisement of our peace was upon Him. And with His stripes we are healed. Through Christ's broken body, make us one. Heal divisions among us. Heal the hurts in our families today. Bring healing to those among us who are sick and suffering. As we eat this bread together, we who are well celebrate our health as a gift of Your grace.

Church can one of the most difficult places in the

world for a believer to be honest about his or her sin. Our concern with what other church people think of us tends to reinforce our pride and intensify our reluctance to admit the truth about ourselves. So during the partaking of the cup, encourage the people to confess their sins and accept God's forgiveness through the shed blood of Christ. Challenge them to leave the Lord's table freshly cleansed from their sins and totally free from guilt.

Remember, more healing and forgiveness are likely to come to God's people through the meaningful celebration of communion than from the last ten minutes of an over-extended sermon.

Through baptism and communion we are reminded of God's eternal promise to redeem and sustain His family. And we are reminded of our covenant relationship with each other in the body of Christ. Baptism celebrates our death to sin and new life in Christ. Communion reminds us of our utter dependence on Christ for our strength and redemption. The wise pastor will recognize the importance of maintaining a strong and healthy emphasis on both of these ordinances in the life of the church.

Suggested Readings—Chapter Five

Ole E. Borgen, *John Wesley on the Sacraments* (Zondervan, 1986).

Donald Bridge and David Phypers, *Communion: The Meal That Unites?* (Shaw Publishers, 1983).

Alec J. Langford, *Invitations to Communion* (Christian Board of Publication, 1986).

Philip H. Pfatteicher, *Foretaste of the Feast to Come: Devotions on Holy Communion* (Augsburg, 1987).

Ceil and Moishe Rosen, *Christ in the Passover* (Moody, 1978).

Caring for Marriages in the Family of God

Only a generation ago, Americans commonly regarded marriage as a sacred institution. The U.S. Supreme Court spoke of marriage as "more than a mere contract," a "holy estate," a "sacred obligation," the "foundation of the family and society, without which there would be neither civilization nor progress."

But since the 1950s, these traditional concepts of marriage have come under increasingly severe attack. So-called no-fault divorce laws, palimony suits and other legal reforms reflect the growing secularization of the institution of marriage.

A new emphasis on individual property rights and sexual privacy rights has further eroded the moral basis of marriage and the family and has created such legal controversies as surrogate motherhood, teenage abortion without parental consent, and distribution of contraceptives through the public schools.

How should the church respond to these attacks on marriage? How can the church help people maintain a biblical approach to marriage in such a secularized and materialistic society?

First, the church has many ways of indirectly communicating the distinction between secular ideas of marriage and those found in Scripture. In preaching, in conducting marriage ceremonies, in dedicating or baptizing infants, and in daily interaction with parishioners, the pastor can contrast biblical and secular ideals of marriage.

Second, the governing body of the local church can express this contrast through its policies regarding the use of church facilities for weddings and receptions.

Finally, wherever marriage is referred to in the life of the church, from membership requirements through the educational curricula of all its departments, care should be taken to distinguish Christian marriage from secular marriage.

Pastoral Communication

The pastor has a responsibility to affirm the authority of the church over Christian marriage. In fulfillment of this responsibility to God and to the church, the pastor should help every couple gain a clear understanding of the Christian view of marriage.

In a society where marriage is increasingly being seen

as a private and secular affair, the role of the pastor is unfortunately becoming more and more peripheral to the marriage ceremony. He is becoming a mere functionary. Couples view the pastor as their agent in making their marriage what they want it to be. Their ideas of marriage have been shaped largely by the popular romantic ideas of secular culture. *Bride's* magazine, "The Love Boat" and soap operas provide idealistic dreams of marriage which contradict Scripture. In this dream world there is no place for the church's authority over marriage.

In some instances, couples simply present their own wedding ceremony to the pastor or insist on editing his. They are offended if they cannot use the music they want, regardless of how secular the lyrics may be. Lyrics like "We've only just begun to live, white lace and promises, a kiss for luck and we're on our way" replace "Heavenly Father, hear us as we pray, here at Thine altar on our wedding day."

How does something so ridiculous happen? It happens because couples are ignorant of the theology of marriage. Even Christian couples are often unaware of the theological nature of marriage and the marriage ceremony. After all, where is the theology of marriage regularly taught in one's church life? Often the couple's only exposure to the theology of Christian marriage comes in premarital counseling or in a preparation-for-marriage class. That is too little, too late.

Couples with a secularized and individualistic world view tend to disregard the authority of the church over their marriage. Instead, they assert their rights to appropriate the church sanctuary as a stage for their wedding. They view the pastor as a culturally approved agent for performing their ceremony. And they see the ceremony as their way of expressing their love for each other.

Why do pastors go along with this? Some pastors may not be aware of the subtle secular assimilation of marriage. They may assume that the democratic thing to do is to permit each couple to tailor the marriage ceremony to fit their own individual tastes. Other pastors may be aware of the secular encroachment but fear the political consequences in the church if they do not permit a particular couple to alter the marriage ceremony. Still other pastors may view themselves as mere agents of the state, and therefore see no theological problem at all in abdicating their control of the ceremony.

In any event, once the pastor permits the secularization of the marriage ceremony, he should be prepared to live with the consequences in the lives of his church family. After all, if a couple will not respect the authority of the church over their marriage ceremony, what is the likelihood that they will respect the authority of the church over their family?

Obviously, this problem cannot be cured overnight. However, by adopting a combination of immediate and long-range approaches, a much healthier attitude toward marriage can be reaffirmed. Here are some places you can begin.

Pulpit Ministry

In our secular climate, Christians need to be reminded

frequently of the covenantal and community obligations of marriage. The early church fathers considered the marriage of a believer to have such a powerful influence on the entire Christian community that they required pastoral approval of every believer's mate choice. This approval was not casually granted. A couple had to demonstrate their compatibility in order to be given permission to marry.

Few of us want to return to this degree of ecclesial control. Nevertheless, marriage is a theological statement, and the church needs to reassert its role in this crucial area of life.

Couples need to be taught that they are accountable for the stewardship of their marriage, not only to God but also to the body of Christ. The divorce of a Christian couple affects the entire body of believers—married and single.

> If one part suffers, every part suffers with it;
> if one part is honored, every part rejoices with
> it (1 Cor. 12:26).

When the ideal of marriage as a lifetime commitment begins to erode within a community, it becomes easier for dissatisfied couples to seek divorce. This compromises the commitment with which single people approach marriage.

One of the most effective ways of teaching your theology of marriage is through the sermon. How often do you preach on marriage and the family? How many times a year do you preach on the importance of commitment and promise-keeping?

We frequently hear sermons on God's faithfulness in keeping His promises to us. We are often reminded of the importance of our faithfulness in keeping promises made to God. But how often do we hear sermons addressing the importance of keeping our promises to each other? Yet it is precisely the ability to commit to covenantal relationships—to keep the promises we have made to each other—that lies at the very heart of a healthy marriage and family.

Examples of the crucial role this kind of commitment plays in establishing healthy family ties can be found throughout Scripture.

The survival of the human race can be traced to the commitment Noah made to God and his family. What would have happened to Lot and his family had it not been for the love and commitment of his uncle Abraham? Only Jacob's commitment to Rachel could keep him peaceful while in Laban's employment for fourteen years. And even when Jacob was deceived into marrying Leah, he was just as committed to providing for her and her children as he was for Rachel and her offspring.

The New Testament begins with the commitment of Joseph to Mary, even after he learned that she was pregnant. Zechariah and Elizabeth, out of their commitment to God and each other, gave birth to one of the world's greatest prophets, John the Baptist. Aquila and Priscilla, tentmakers in Corinth, out of their spiritual commitment established a church in their home and taught Apollos the more perfect way of the Lord.

Such rich biblical resources provide much-needed

sermon material for reminding our selfish generation of the long-term benefits to be reaped from relationships built on lifetime commitment, loyalty and love.

Conducting Marriages

Early in his ministry the pastor will confront some difficult questions about performing marriage ceremonies. He may ask himself, Am I morally obligated to perform the marriage ceremony of any couple who seeks my services? How is my office unique among others in the community empowered to perform marriages? Which marriages are more appropriately performed by nonclergy? What is my obligation to an unbelieving couple who ask me to perform their marriage ceremony? Should unbelievers be married in the sanctuary of the church? How should I deal with the marriage ceremony of unbelieving children of faithful members of the church? Should I perform a ceremony uniting a believer to an unbeliever?

This list of questions by no means exhausts the concerns a conscientious pastor wrestles with. Unfortunately, many pastors fail to deal with the difficult issues raised by these questions. Instead, they allow politically sensitive circumstances in the congregation to override theological concerns.

As a result, insistent couples and their families are permitted to make theological decisions about marriage that should be made only by the pastor. Over a period of years, this approach results in such gross theological confusion and inconsistencies in judgment that the average parishioner is unable to understand the difference between the sacred and the secular approach to marriage.

Thus, the pastor who clearly defines the circumstances under which he will officiate at weddings and consistently abides by this position has gone a long way toward helping his congregation understand the difference between secular and sacred marriage. This is not a simple task. It requires commitment to Scripture, clarity of thought, courage of heart and patient consistency in application.

Premarital Counseling

If the church does not assume responsibility for preparing couples for Christian marriage, who will? Divorce statistics attest that families are failing as a dependable source of training for marriage. Government institutions offer couples little or no help; more training is required for a driver's license than for a marriage license. And any training that is offered by public institutions, such as schools, must be free from any spiritual values.

This makes it all the more urgent that the church implement effective programs of premarital counseling. With rare exceptions, all couples married by the pastor should be required to complete his premarital counseling program.

Here are some suggested goals for an effective premarital counseling program:

• Provide the couple with a biblical view of marriage.

• Encourage each partner to resolve any concerns or misgivings he or she may have about the marriage.

• Explore the couple's expectations of marriage and

modify them where necessary.

• Provide the couple with basic skills in marital communication.

• Be sure the couple is entering marriage with adequate and accurate information about sex.

• Explain the theological significance of the marriage ceremony.

• Clarify plans for the rehearsal and wedding.

"Remarital" Counseling

Those remarrying may be in greater need of counseling than those being married for the first time. They are often facing a more complicated task than in their first marriage. Not only must they make the normal adjustments involved in separating from their families and becoming attached to each other, they must also deal with unresolved issues from their previous marriage. And, of course, they face other complex issues created by any children brought into their new marriage.

Unfortunately, many couples who are remarrying assume they have nothing to gain from premarital counseling. They may have had premarital counseling before they married the first time. Besides, they were married; they know what it's all about. In addition, going for premarital counseling the second time may intensify any remaining guilt over the failure of the previous marriage. So this requirement may seem condescending to some and threatening to others.

Thus the pastor may find it effective to provide "remarital" counseling in addition to "premarital" counseling. He can explain to remarrying couples that this program is different from premarital counseling and has been designed specifically to meet their needs. (In larger churches, both the premarital and remarital counseling programs can be offered regularly as electives through the Christian education department.) All remarrying couples should be required to complete the remarital counseling program—regardless of whether their previous marriage was ended by divorce or by death.

Here are some suggestions for a remarital counseling program for those whose previous marriage was ended by divorce:

• Insist that both individuals be at least one year beyond their divorce before entering remarital counseling.

• Help the couple carefully and prayerfully explore the emotional residue each person may be bringing from previous relationships into the new relationship.

For example, there will be a tendency for each partner to be overly sensitive in the areas where he or she was hurt in former relationships. So each is likely to overreact to the slightest hint of these behaviors in the other. Identifying these potential problem areas will help both partners better understand themselves and each other.

• When no children are involved, the remarrying couple should consider the following:

1. Have you reflected on ways you contributed to the failure of your previous marriage? (Suggest a book each can read about the opposite sex that is written by a member of the opposite sex.)

2. Have you thought of ways you might have

anticipated unacceptable aspects of your previous marriage?

3. Before you married your former spouse, did you talk with anyone who knew him or her, who could have provided you with a more objective view?

4. How familiar were you with his or her family before you married?

5. How have you approached your selection of this mate differently from the way you chose your previous one?

6. Are you prepared to accept your new mate without prejudging him or her on the basis of unpleasant experiences with your previous spouse?

• When children from a previous marriage are involved, their issues need to explored.

If the children are of preschool age, it is not necessary for them to participate in the discussion. Older children, however, should be involved in at least one remarital counseling session. They should be encouraged to express candidly their feelings about their parent's prospective partner and about the possibility of their parent's marriage with no fear of retaliation by the couple. Suggestions should be made for structuring the new family relationships so that everyone's physical and emotional needs will be considered and respected.

A commitment should be elicited from the couple and the children to continue meeting with the pastor (or a competent counselor) for the first six to twelve months of the new marriage. Initially, they should meet with the counselor every two weeks. After the first three months, if all is going well, the frequency can be reduced to once a month. This kind of nurturing oversight will prove to be valuable preventive maintenance for which most couples will be extremely grateful.

• Parents who are bringing children from a previous marriage into their relationship should understand that:

The issues between former mates and the children will have to be faced.

1. The role of the stepparents in the lives of the children will need to be determined.

2. The natural parent should likely be the primary disciplinarian. The extent to which children will receive discipline from a stepparent will be determined by the nature of the relationship between them and the stepparent.

3. The couple will have to negotiate rules of the house that each feels are fair and that each will be willing to enforce.

4. Each set of children will need time with their natural parent.

5. The new family will need to find group activities that can give it some identity of its own.

• Specific issues to be explored in remarital counseling with widows or widowers include:

1. How long has it been since the death of the previous spouse?

2. How effectively has the essential grief work been done? Usually, from one to two years is required for the grieving process.

3. Have the dependent children been able to deal with the death of their parent? Are they angry about the possibility of a new spouse assuming their deceased

parent's place in the home?

4. The surviving spouse and children should be reminded of the tendency of memory to retain the pleasant and forget the unpleasant. This will help them avoid temptations to compare the best in the deceased spouse and parent with the worst in the living spouse and stepparent. It will also permit them to build new memories with the present spouse and stepparent without feeling guilty.

5. In some cases, a prenuptial agreement should be considered in order to protect the estate of children whose parent is deceased.

Gaining Board Approval

Once you have defined your premarital and remarital counseling programs, explain them to your board. This will inform them about a very important part of your ministry. It will also gain their support for your insistence that every couple being married in the church go through this preparation.

Having the governing board approve the premarital and remarital counseling programs as official church policy can shield the pastor from political pressure and social awkwardness. He can explain that he is merely carrying out the stated policy of the church.

The Wedding Ceremony

At some point in the ceremony the pastor should remind the couple, their families and their guests of the major differences between Christian marriage and pagan marriage.

Many Americans may be offended by the word "pagan," thinking that our culture is more refined and therefore more divinely acceptable than primitive "heathen" cultures. But the secular or sacred nature of a wedding is not determined by the cultural refinement reflected in the ceremony. Unless a Christian couple recognizes the lordship of Jesus over their marriage, their ceremony is as secular as those married by civil authorities and as pagan as those in tribal societies.

Christian marriage is not simply a civil contract ratified amid ecclesiastical trappings. Marriage is an extension of God's image in humankind. Just as the creation of Adam in trinity of being (body, soul and spirit) reflected the divine trinity (Father, Son and Holy Spirit), so the Christian husband and wife are to relate to each other as Christ relates to the church. Just as the Father, the Holy Spirit and the only begotten Son live in unbroken unity in heaven, so a husband and wife and any children born to them are to live in unbroken unity on earth.

This distinction needs to be made not only for the benefit of the couple, but also for the sake of everyone in attendance at the wedding. If the ceremony does not announce this with sufficient clarity, the pastor should embellish it.

When children from previous marriages are brought into a new marriage, they should be included in the vows. The ceremony should include references to those understandings reached in remarital counseling. For example, "I, _____ , take you, _____ , to be my wedded wife and I take your children to love and to cherish as members of our family.'' The pastor may also want to include a pledge of support from each child: ''_____ , you are entering into a new family. Will you give this new family your trust, love and affection?''

Reinforce the Importance of Marriage

The occasion of infant baptism or baby dedication affords the pastor another opportunity to contrast the secular and sacred approach to marriage. To the Christian community, babies are not mere accidents of evolution. They are divine gifts entrusted to the parents and to the Christian community. This sacred dimension of life must never be compromised.

Care should be taken to present the baby as a potential channel of God's grace to the next generation. The parents and the Christian community should be challenged to be good stewards of this new life entrusted to them. This is an excellent opportunity to remind the parents and the congregation of the tremendous difference being born into a Christian community can make in a person's life.

The child born into a Christian home and nurtured by a Christian community is more likely to discover and fulfill his or her potential than one raised by secular or pagan parents. The difference should be in the quality of life modeled for the child by his parents and the Christian community. This difference transcends national and cultural boundaries.

Remind the adults of the impact their example has on the children and youth of the congregation. Remind children and youth of the blessings of growing up in a Christian home. As you challenge parents to model the Christian life for their children, you can also remind the children to honor and obey their parents. In this way, infant baptisms and baby dedications can be a time when everyone rededicates himself to the Christian ideals of marriage and family.

Informal Pastoral Communication

Much of the pastor's influence over the congregation can be traced to his informal times with them—after-church snacks, hospital calls, home visits, church picnics, holiday get-togethers. In such informal moments, people are often more open than in more structured church settings.

Opportunities to communicate needed spiritual guidance are often forfeited to social trivia. Of course, as pastor you want people to know you as a human being. But they also need to know you as a spiritual guide. So take a few minutes now and then in informal conversation to stress the importance of families recognizing Christ as the head of their home.

Christians are people of commitment and promise-keeping. Our relationships are not merely contractual. They are covenantal. They cannot be bargained away. Our friendships should be more loyal and our marriages more sacred than those of the secular world. We are not our own; we were bought with a price—the redeeming blood of Christ. We belong to Him. And because we belong to Him, we belong to each other.

Suggested Readings—Chapter Six

Jay E. Adams, *Marriage, Divorce and Remarriage in the Bible* (Zondervan, 1986).

James L. Christensen, *The Minister's Marriage Handbook* (Revell, 1974).

John Killinger, *Contemporary Wedding Services* (Westminster Press).

Richard P. Olson, *Help for Remarried Couples and Families* (Judson, 1984).

Gary Smalley, *For Better or for Best: A Valuable Guide to Knowing, Understanding and Loving Your Husband* (Zondervan, 1982).

Gary Smalley, *If He Only Knew: A Valuable Guide to Knowing, Understanding and Loving Your Wife* (Zondervan, 1982).

SEVEN

Redemptive Ministries: Extending the Family

The natural family was designed by God to procreate, nurture, strengthen and sustain life from birth to death. In much the same way, the church, as the spiritual family of God, has been designed to evangelize, nurture, disciple, strengthen and sustain the life of God's children.

Just as the primary purpose of the family is procreation, so the primary purpose of the church is evangelism. Sadly, some couples suffer the pain and disappointment of a childless marriage. But they can adopt a child or children and thus complete God's purpose for their marriage. Nevertheless, theologically speaking, procreation is the primary function of the family. We should never waver from this vital principle.

Once children have been born, of course, they need to be cared for and trained to live productive lives. This relationship between reaching and teaching is reflected in the accounts of the Great Commission as recorded in the Gospels of Mark and Matthew:

> Go into all the world and preach the good news to all creation. Whoever believes and is baptized will be saved, but whoever does not believe will be condemned (Mark 16:15-16).

> Go and make disciples of all nations, baptizing them in the name of the Father and of the Son and of the Holy Spirit, and teaching them to obey everything I have commanded you. And surely I am with you always, to the very end of the age (Matt. 28:19-20).

Mark's passage emphasizes evangelism; Matthew's emphasizes teaching and training. Without taking anything away from its emphasis on evangelism, the church can and should do a better job of nurturing and training the people reached through its evangelistic fervor.

As it is in the church, so should it be with regard to the family. The church and the family are the only institutions in our society that have personal interaction with us from birth to death. Through the fall of our first parents Adam and Eve, Satan has fatally flawed the family's ability to train its offspring to live in perfect obedience to the Word of God. History is filled with examples of families whose spiritual and moral rebellion have brought decay and destruction to succeeding generations.

The ever-present materialism and hedonism of our society offers continuing proof that the flawed character of Adam is still with us. This rebellious attachment to money and self, rather than to God and others, has resulted in the secularization of sex and marriage—which, in turn, has led to a phenomenal breakdown of the family.

The number of single-parent households is increasing twenty times as fast as the number of two-parent families. Evidences of shattered relationships are all about us.

God, through Christ, offers the church as a surrogate spiritual family to minister redemptively to the brokenness of fallen families. This is the hope the church holds for people suffering from fragmented relationships.

Through our spiritual family, we not only are given the hope of eternal reunion in heaven, but we can also learn how to restore many of our relationships in this world. After all, God doesn't just want us to get to heaven; He also wants us to enjoy the trip!

Applied Theology

If the church is to fulfill its mission to families, it must be equipped with an applied theology that meets today's needs. Although dogmatic theology is essential for keeping the church free from heresy, people desperately need an applied theology to help them "make the Word flesh" (see John 1:14) in their daily lives. Discovering an applied theology that works will engender deeper commitment to the church's dogmatic theology. People will cling more tenaciously to a biblical theology that makes a difference in the home and on the job than to one that merely maintains denominational distinctions.

A healthy applied theology enables the child of God to manifest the Word of God in attitudes and behavior— it helps the child of God make the Word flesh. The Bible works when it is applied to the real issues of life. Nowhere is this more evident than in the life and ministry of Jesus.

Jesus met people at their point of need. He talked with the woman of Samaria about her marital chaos. He dealt with Zaccheus about his dishonesty in tax collecting. He faced Mary Magdalene with the problems prostitution had brought into her life. He confronted the rich young ruler with his love of money. He fed the hungry, healed the sick and blessed the children.

Although the basic spiritual needs of people remain the same today as they were in the day of Jesus, the social context of each generation is unique. Were Jesus coming to minister in person to the people of our generation, He wouldn't sit by wells or look for people sitting in trees. But He would still address the moral consequences of broken marriages and cohabitation; He would still face the ugly issues of pornography and promiscuity; He would still confront the evils of materialism. And, of course, He would still take time to feed the hungry, heal the sick and bless the children.

Traditionally, the church has taught people the ought-tos of life. People know they "ought to" repent, confess, forgive, lay aside bitterness, be tenderhearted, cast their cares on Christ, put off the old man and put on the new, honor their husbands, love their wives, obey their parents, not let the sun go down upon their wrath, and so on. However, church people are often left not knowing how to do what they know they ought to do.

People in our congregations are crying out for help in making their faith relevant to the practical issues of their lives. They want to take their faith home with them and practice it during the week. But they need help bridging the gap between dogmatic theology and applied theology.

The church's challenge is to operationalize the ought-tos of its dogmatic theology into the how-tos of an applied theology. From the cradle roll to the senior citizens' group, the departments and programs of the church must minister practically to the needs of God's family at all ages and phases of life.

The Word of God is timeless in its relevance to human need. Today, the church needs programs and materials that relate the truths of the Bible to the needs of our generation. In some cases this may be done by modifying existing programs and editing existing materials. However, it is almost certain that new programs and materials will need to be developed as well.

Here are some program ideas for operationalizing an applied theology for contemporary family needs. The first group is redemptive in nature. They are designed to heal the hurts of the brokenhearted and bereaved. The second group is preventive in nature. It is intended to help people anticipate the predictable demands of life and to equip them with Christian coping skills.

Redemptive Programs

Redemption has to do with deliverance from Satan's power. The deliverance Jesus provides is eternal, but it is temporal as well. Consider the following biblical passages:

> The thief comes only to steal and kill and destroy; I have come that they may have life, and have it to the full (John 10:10).

> For he has rescued us from the dominion of darkness and brought us into the kingdom of the Son he loves, in whom we have redemption, the forgiveness of sins (Col. 1:13-14).

The redemptive benefits of the kingdom of God are not all delayed until ''the sweet by and by.'' Both these passages refer to redemptive benefits in this life—here and now. Programs that are truly redemptive minimize the destructive impact of sin on people's lives and help restore them to a peaceful, joyful life in Christ.

Perhaps no group of people needs this kind of help more than single-parent and divorced families. By single-parent families I mean those headed by women who were never legally married to the father of their children or by divorced women whose ex-husbands do not visit or support their children. By divorced families I mean those in which the father does regularly visit and support the children. In both of these situations, mothers carry a disproportionate share of the parental responsibilities and often feel overwhelmed by them.

Through creative use of the church's most valuable

resource—its own people—redemptive benefits can be brought to single-parent and divorced families. Simply by extending themselves in love, healthy families can have a fulfilling ministry to some very special people in the family of God.

Single-Parent and Divorced Families

Within most congregations there are both single and divorced parents. In many cases these people are living at a distance from their own families, and they need help raising their children. Within the very same congregations, there are usually older couples who either have no children or who live at a distance from their children and grandchildren. The church family can offer both groups an opportunity to meet each other's needs.

Why not design a program that would encourage older couples to adopt a single-parent or divorced family for a year? Invite those interested in participating to a kick-off dinner at the church. Explain the program and pair up the older couples with the single-parent or divorced families as seems most suitable.

During the following year, the two families might get together for a potluck dinner once a month. Since both families are likely to be on limited budgets, such an arrangement would allow them to share the expense. Each family could be responsible for part of the menu.

This would give single-parent and divorced families an invaluable opportunity to observe a healthy marriage and to experience wholesome family times. In many cases, the two families will establish an ongoing relationship. The older couple could make it a point to remember the children's birthdays and perhaps baby-sit for the single parent a couple of times a month. The single parent could do some errands or household tasks for the older couple.

The role of the church should be limited to helping the families find each other and giving them suggestions for establishing a healthy relationship. The older people should be cautioned about becoming overly intrusive in the single parent's family. The single parent should be cautioned about becoming overly dependent on the older couple.

As you can see, such a relationship would provide many benefits to everyone involved. At the end of a year, families could opt out of the program, choose to continue for another year with the same family or be paired with another.

Lonely Senior Citizens

Senior citizens, especially those who are single and who live at a distance from their families, are another group whose needs could be addressed by families. Almost every congregation has a number of senior citizens who are lonely and feel left out. Why not present younger couples in the church with an opportunity to extend their family to include a senior member of the congregation? They could invite the senior for dinner once or twice a month, remember his or her birthday, and include him or her in other family celebrations.

Once this kind of relationship is established, family members will discover other ways to extend themselves to the senior in Christian love.

College Students Away from Home

If your church is located near a college campus, you have the opportunity to minister to another group which needs to feel included in the family of God—college students. Encourage couples with children in high school or college to invite the students into their homes and occasionally include them in the family's weekend plans. By this simple act of hospitality, lifelong friendships can be formed.

Redemptive Ministries: Care Group

The rapid growth of the early church was rooted in its commitment to care for one another. Luke records,

> All the believers were together and had every-thing in common. Selling their possessions and goods, they gave to anyone as he had need. Every day they continued to meet together in the temple courts. They broke bread in their homes and ate together with glad and sincere hearts, praising God and enjoying the favor of all the people. And the Lord added to their number daily those who were being saved (Acts 2:44-47).

This intense mission of world evangelism was

temporarily interrupted in order for the apostles to be sure that Christian widows and orphans were being cared for properly.

> In those days when the number of disciples was increasing, the Grecian Jews among them complained against the Hebraic Jews because their widows were being overlooked in the daily distribution of food. So the Twelve gathered all the disciples together and said, "It would not be right for us to neglect the ministry of the word of God in order to wait on tables. Brothers, choose seven men from among you who are known to be full of the Spirit and wisdom. We will turn this responsibility over to them and will give our attention to prayer and the ministry of the word."
>
> This proposal pleased the whole group. They chose Stephen, a man full of faith and of the Holy Spirit; also Philip, Procorus, Nicanor, Timon, Parmenas, and Nicolas from Antioch, a convert to Judaism. They presented these men to the apostles, who prayed and laid their hands on them.
>
> So the word of God spread. The number of disciples in Jerusalem increased rapidly, and a large number of priests became obedient to the faith (Acts 6:1-7).

God honored the concern of the apostles and deacons for their fellow Christians by enabling the church to be more and more effective in evangelism.

In writing to the churches in Galatia, Paul continued to emphasize the importance of Christians caring for each other:

> Brothers, if someone is caught in a sin, you who are spiritual should restore him gently. But watch yourself, or you also may be tempted. Carry each other's burdens, and in this way you will fulfill the law of Christ. If anyone thinks he is something when he is nothing, he deceives himself.
>
> Do not be deceived: God cannot be mocked. A man reaps what he sows. The one who sows to please his sinful nature, from that nature will reap destruction; the one who sows to please the Spirit, from the Spirit will reap eternal life. Let us not become weary in doing good, for at the proper time we will reap a harvest if we do not give up. Therefore, as we have opportunity, let us do good to all people, especially to those who belong to the family of believers (Gal. 6:1-3; 7-10).

Care and Outreach

Today our hedonistic and materialistic society is producing an increasing number of people who have been hurt and victimized by those they once trusted. Many of these people are turning to the church for help and healing: the divorced, the children of divorce, the bereaved, adults who are former victims of incest or child molestation, the unemployed and those suffering from job displacement (the list goes on and on). The needs represented among these people are many and varied. However, often there are enough people suffering from the same or similar problems to warrant special attention to their particular needs.

Through Christian education electives and small group outreach programs, the church can reach not only its own members, but also other hurting people in the community at large.

Some groups, such as those dealing with the problems of the newly divorced, might be designed primarily to meet the needs of the church family. Other groups, such as those for victims of child molestation and job displacement, might be designed primarily as outreach ministries.

Studies have shown the effectiveness of small groups in supporting people through their recovery from painful life crises. Results also indicate that by using small groups to teach skills for dealing with crisis problems, subsequent physical and emotional damage can be prevented.

In the sixties, a number of pastors began to experiment with small groups as a means for church growth and general pastoral care. Some pastors were able to develop and integrate this kind of small group ministry into the permanent structure of their church. By simply broadening the focus of small group ministry to include special groups for specific needs, compassionate care can be extended to people suffering from common hurts.

Leadership for such groups should be carefully chosen

from among those the Lord has enabled to recover from the problem being addressed by the group. This approach also provides ministry opportunities for those whose previous problems might disqualify them from other areas of leadership.

Those selected should be thoroughly trained in the area of their group's special ministry and in group leadership skills.

The Newly Divorced

Of primary concern to newly divorced parents is the impact of their divorce on their children. The church can respond to this need in three ways:

First, the Christian education department can offer a continuing elective for those who are single again. In fact, that could be the name of the class, Single Again.

Second, classes for the children of newly divorced parents also can be provided by the Christian education department.

Third, as noted earlier, through a program of spiritual adoption, older couples whose children and grandchildren live at a distance from them can be encouraged to take a special interest in single mothers and their children.

Single Again

Although single adults have distinct needs, they do not like to be isolated from the married members of the congregation. When they are divided from other church members during the Sunday school hour, they tend to feel stigmatized. Therefore, the single-again class should meet at a different time from the regular services of the church.

This group needs to be distinguished from other singles. Many churches have yet to recognize that there are more than forty-five million single adults in our country—constituting almost twenty percent of the population—and that this group is widely diverse in nature. The total single population includes the never-married, the unmarried with children, the divorced and the widowed. Each of these subgroups has very different needs. Ages within each subgroup may vary from eighteen to eighty. Any church wanting to provide meaningful ministry to singles should bear in mind the diverse nature of this population.

In some areas churches cooperate in a community-wide ministry to singles early Sunday morning, before the Sunday school or worship hour. Other churches provide singles' ministry on Sunday evening. When the church holds regular Sunday evening services, the single-again group could meet after the service or at some other time during the week.

The curriculum for a group of this nature should include: a theology of marriage, divorce and remarriage; re-establishing yourself as a single person; special issues for single parents; sex and the single adult. (See references at the end of the chapter for suggested curriculum materials.)

Children of the Newly Divorced

Just like their parents, children of the newly divorced

need special attention. And, just like their parents, they don't want to be stigmatized. They want to fit in with other young people in the church.

One way to accommodate both of these needs—for special attention and for fitting in with other young people—is to arrange a special meeting for them during the time when their parents are attending the single-again meeting.

Ideally, this class should be taught by a healthy Christian adult who was raised by a divorced parent. Another suitable teaching candidate would be a divorced Christian parent whose children are raised and living healthy adult lives. Curriculum for this class should help answer such questions as:

- Why did my mom and dad divorce?
- Should Christians divorce?
- What does God think of divorce?
- Should I pray that my parents will get back together?
- How can I love both of my parents when they don't love each other any longer?
- Since my parents divorced, am I more likely to divorce?
- How can I protect my future marriage from divorce?

Blended Families

Many children of newly divorced parents will find themselves in blended families. A blended family consists of at least one spouse who brings children from a previous marriage into the new marriage. Although this kind of family is becoming increasingly common, little has been done to minister to their unique needs.

Much like the single-again group, blended families will not want to be separated from the church family during regular teaching and service times. They, too, will best be served by a program that meets at a separate time.

What is blending? The best illustration I have heard came from a woman involved in a blended family. She told me she was praying for an understanding of how she, her husband and their two sets of children could relate most compatibly to each other. As she did, she began to see the life of each person in the family as a container of liquid being poured into one large container. This helped her understand that even though each member of their blended family would continue to live as individuals, their lives also would continue together in the larger container of the family and could never be entirely separate from each other again.

Here are some of the primary issues blended families must face:

• **The children come with the marriage.** A person cannot, on the one hand, be married to someone who has children and, on the other hand, be divorced from those children. Realizing that you are joined to your partner's body and that their children are products of his or her body can help you accept your "marriage" to the children. A husband who loves his wife and wants to possess her body but rejects her children, which are the products of her body, needs to understand what a contradiction this is. The same is true for the wife.

• **Jealousy is a big hurdle to overcome.** In the beginning of the marriage, the partners tend to be jealous of the former spouse and of the children. The children tend to be jealous of their parent's new partner.

One of the first things the couple must do is to reassure the children that the marriage is not going to take their parent away from them. Allowing each child (or set of children) private time with their natural parent each week will help toward this goal. Of course, so that the new family unit can be gradually defined, common rules of the house have to be negotiated and enforced by the parents. Fun times together as a whole new family will help to speed up this process of identity.

The husband needs to reassure the wife that his love for her is strong enough to allow her the freedom she needs to communicate with her children's father regarding parental concerns. The wife needs to give the husband the same reassurance. Both partners should be careful to carry out communications with former spouses in such a way as to strengthen this kind of mutual trust.

Although neither partner can control what a former spouse may do, each can control his or her reaction to those circumstances.

Learning to Live Again

Helping people through the grieving process is a vital ministry of the church. The Christian's hope of resurrection is a source of great comfort and strength; even so, separation from loved ones because of death still stings. Even though Jesus knew He was about to raise Lazarus from the dead, He identified with the grief of Lazarus's family and friends and wept with them over their loss (see John 11:1-36).

The Bible clearly makes caring for widows and

orphans a primary responsibility of the Christian community. "Religion that God our Father accepts as pure and faultless is this: to look after orphans and widows in their distress and to keep oneself from being polluted by the world" (James 1:27).

In spite of this biblical admonition, the bereaved often feel neglected by the church. When asked how their local church might serve them better, Christians in one survey placed top priority on more pastoral attention following the death of a loved one.

Typically, a pastor will call on a family immediately following a death. He will attend the wake, conduct the funeral and make a follow-up visit. Yet most families can benefit from personal pastoral care for three to six months following the loss of a loved one. (The length of care will be determined by the nature of the death.)

One way of giving additional support to those recovering from the loss of a loved one is through a "learning to live again" care group. If one congregation does not have a sufficient need for this kind of group, a cooperative effort of several churches can be launched.

A local church may also want to launch such a care group as an outreach ministry to the unchurched. An appropriately worded announcement through the local media can be a good way of bringing the program to the public's attention.

Ideally, the group should meet twice a month. Since all those in grief will share certain common reactions to their loss, the group's curriculum should cover these areas:

- **Mourning inevitably involves both anxiety and**

denial. These are normal reactions to death. Healthy grieving will move a person beyond this over a period of several days. If a person has not been able to dispose of the personal belongings of the deceased within four to six weeks after the funeral, for example, they may need special attention.

• **Feelings of dejection, disorganization and depletion of energies are common.** A person in grief may have difficulty sleeping for several weeks. Care should be taken to avoid becoming overly dependent on sleep medication during this time.

• **Expressing grief is essential to the recovery process.** The privacy this requires tends to aggravate the loneliness that comes as a normal consequence of the death of a loved one. Participation in the care group can help alleviate this burden.

• **Special attention should be given those whose grief is exacerbated by unusually tragic circumstances.** For grown children to bury their parents is expected. But parents do not expect to bury their children. This kind of premature death intensifies grief. Homicide, suicide and accidental death are other examples that confront the bereaved with unusually difficult grief.

• **Especially in cases of tragic death, mourners should be helped to avoid asking why.** The family inevitably wrestles with this question, but it is unanswerable. As soon as possible, the bereaved ones should be helped to shift their focus to an answerable question: How can I find God in my tragedy?

This kind of explanation is called a theodicy. Perhaps one of the most important functions of a care group for the bereaved is to help people discover a positive theodicy for their loss.

Robert Wuthnow, in "Religion and Bereavement: A Conceptual Framework" (*Journal for the Scientific Study of Religion*, 1980), lists five common theodicies that people resort to in explaining their tragedies:

1. People may blame or question the mercy of God.

2. People may view tragedy as a punishment for the wrongdoing of survivors.

3. People may assume the events are intended to serve a good and useful purpose.

4. People may see suffering as primarily a state of mind that can be influenced by how one defines a situation.

5. People may regard death as fatalistic, coincidental or solely in causal terms.

Obviously, some of these theodicies are detrimental and some are therapeutic. Helping members of the group avoid destructive theodicies and adopt therapeutic ones should be a major goal for those learning to live again.

Learning to Love Again

There is a growing need among Christians for ministry to adult victims of child molestation. Ongoing cases of child molestation should be dealt with in private counseling and in cooperation with local child protection agencies. But adults who carry within them the haunting memories of this tragedy can be effectively helped through care group ministry.

Because of the personal nature of this problem, meetings should be held at times and places to provide maximum confidentiality. An ad in the classified section of the local newspaper or on cable television, with a private telephone number or post office box, would be appropriate ways of advertising the meeting.

Because of the delicate and serious nature of the issues involved, the learning-to-love-again group should be led by someone with professional training in Christian counseling. The following issues should be addressed:

• **Memories of past experiences.** Healing for these hurtful memories should be sought by "praying through." This means using prayer to drain traumatic memories of their debilitating effects. Four steps are involved:

1. *Talk to God honestly about what hurts you.* Because of the sexual (and sometimes perverse) nature of these memories, people often feel they cannot even talk to God about them. Since they are embarrassed to share these hurts with anyone else, they feel increasingly stigmatized. By helping people discover that they can talk to God about these experiences, the mystique of the secret is broken and the healing process begins.

2. *Express your feelings to God in prayer.* Beneath these memories are feelings of anger, resentment, bitterness, fear and guilt. Many people are uncomfortable even thinking about expressing such feelings to God. By providing them with the model of David's imprecatory psalms (for example, Psalms 55-59), you can inspire them to be open with God about these secret feelings. Since people often become quite emotional in praying through, they should be encouraged to pursue this task in private.

3. *Wait for God to comfort you.* After a person is

emotionally spent in prayer, he or she should learn to wait on God for some word of comfort. This may come in the form of an appropriate passage of Scripture or may consist of reflecting back on some previous time of despair and being reassured that God's care will be adequate now, just as it was adequate then.

4. *Praise God for His comfort.* Spending a few moments in praise can help to maximize the impact of God's comfort.

• **Issues of forgiveness.** Most memories must be prayed through several times before their pain subsides. Praying through is like peeling an onion—you take it layer by layer and cry a lot.

Often, victims of child molestation and incest attempt to forgive their offenders without first dealing with their anger. Perhaps this is because we are taught we must forgive our enemies, regardless of our feelings, if we want God to forgive us.

Certainly there is no doubt about the believer's obligation to forgive. Jesus is very clear in His teaching on the subject:

> For if you forgive men when they sin against you, your heavenly Father will also forgive you. But if you do not forgive men their sins, your Father will not forgive your sins (Matt. 6:14,15).

> Then Peter came to Jesus and asked, "Lord, how many times shall I forgive my brother when he sins against me? Up to seven times?"
> Jesus answered, "I tell you, not seven times, but seventy-seven times.

"Therefore, the kingdom of heaven is like a king who wanted to settle accounts with his servants. As he began the settlement, a man who owed him ten thousand talents was brought to him. Since he was not able to pay, the master ordered that he and his wife and his children and all that he had be sold to repay the debt.

"The servant fell on his knees before him. 'Be patient with me,' he begged, 'and I will pay back everything.' The servant's master took pity on him, canceled the debt and let him go.

"But when that servant went out, he found one of his fellow servants who owed him a hundred denarii. He grabbed him and began to choke him. 'Pay back what you owe me!' he demanded.

"His fellow servant fell to his knees and begged him, 'Be patient with me, and I will pay you back.'

"But he refused. Instead, he went off and had the man thrown into prison until he could pay the debt. When the other servants saw what had happened, they were greatly distressed and went and told their master everything that had happened.

"Then the master called the servant in. 'You wicked servant,' he said, 'I canceled all that debt of yours because you begged me to. Shouldn't you have had mercy on your fellow servant just as I had on you?' In anger his master turned him over to the jailers to be tortured, until he should pay back all he owed.

"This is how my heavenly Father will treat
each of you unless you forgive your brother from
your heart" (Matt. 18:21-35).

The difference between *willingness* to forgive and
readiness to forgive needs to be distinguished. A person should be willing to forgive immediately. But
readiness to forgive often requires some preparation.

By insisting that people forgive before they are ready
to forgive, you only frustrate the healing process. Until
people have been helped to surrender the hurt and the
anger involved with their pain, only a pretense of forgiveness is possible. But once they have been pressured
into a public confession of forgiveness, the hurt and pain
are trapped within their minds or spirits.

I call this scabby forgiveness. There is an appearance
of forgiveness, but if you peel back the memory of the
event you will discover hurt, anger, bitterness, hostil-
ity and resentment still there. This infection of the soul
must be drained.

People cannot forgive their offenders until they deal
with their feelings about having been violated and
deprived of the innocence of childhood. One effective
way of getting at these feelings is for the person to write
a letter to the offender—a letter they never intend to
mail. Since such an accumulation of feelings is not likely
to surface during any one particular time of writing, the
letter should be written over an extended period of time.

When the letter is finished, the person should be
encouraged to use it during steps 1 and 2 of praying through. Once the remaining issues have been
prayed through, the person needs to find some way of

destroying the letter. By doing so, they can offer up symbolically this part of their past to the Lord and put these feelings behind them. Then, with the help of the Lord, they are finally ready to forgive their offender and close this part of their past.

• **A theology of the body.** Victims of incest and child molestation desperately need a healthy biblical approach to sexuality. They need to know why God made us sexual persons. The first lesson in my series *Raising Healthy Children in a Sexually Sick World* (Emerge Ministries) addresses this need.

Unhealthy body attitudes need to be replaced by healthy ones reflected in the Scriptures. The body is the temple within which we communicate with God (see 1 Cor. 6:19-20). Here is where we experience the righteousness, peace and joy of His presence (see Rom. 14:17).

The body is also our love gift to our spouse in marriage (see 1 Cor. 7:2-5). Within the sacredness of this lifetime commitment we give ourselves in life and love. Thus, we are bonded to each other.

We know that the healing process is complete when the former victim of incest and child molestation is able to express these biblical attitudes and behaviors in marriage. A testimony to this before the group solidifies the healing and encourages hope in others.

Providers

When God created Adam, He gave him a job to do. ''The Lord God took the man and put him in the Garden of Eden to work it and take care of it'' (Gen. 2:15).

Work is part of man's mission in life. Paul reminds the Thessalonian Christians of how deeply this work ethic is embedded in the Christian faith.

> Even when we were with you, we gave you this rule: ''If a man will not work, he shall not eat.''
> We hear that some among you are idle. They are not busy; they are busybodies. Such people we command and urge in the Lord Jesus Christ to settle down and earn the bread they eat. And as for you, brothers, never tire of doing what is right (2 Thess. 3:10-13).

As long as job opportunities are plentiful, people can be fairly confronted with this admonition. But in times of economic recession or in geographical pockets of unemployment the church must emphasize responding compassionately to victims of unemployment.

Few blows deal greater damage to a person's self-respect than unemployment. Today, since multi-national corporations are seeking cheaper international labor forces, men who are production workers are more likely to be victims of long-term unemployment than any other group. This kind of job displacement brings tremendous pressure to bear upon marriage and family relationships.

On the other hand, service industry jobs have increased. Traditionally, women have been trained for these jobs. Therefore, job opportunities for women are much more available in most communities. This can make it difficult for wives to understand why it is so hard for their husbands to find work.

Although the government places a welfare net under the unemployed, this in itself can be a regular reminder of lost self-respect. In any case, it is seldom adequate to meet a family's needs.

How can the church respond compassionately to members who are caught in these circumstances? James reminds us of our first obligation:

> Suppose a brother or sister is without clothes and daily food. If one of you says to him, ''Go, I wish you well; keep warm and well fed,'' but does nothing about his physical needs, what good is it? (James 2:15,16).

A portion of the church's home mission budget should be devoted to emergency relief for unemployed members. Although criteria need to be defined which will permit the distribution of this help on an equitable basis, care should be taken to protect the dignity of the recipients. Jesus instructs us as to how our alms should be given:

> Be careful not to do your ''acts of righteousness'' before men, to be seen by them. If you do, you will have no reward from your Father in heaven.
>
> So when you give to the needy, do not announce it with trumpets, as the hypocrites do in the synagogues and on the streets, to be honored by men. I tell you the truth, they have received their reward in full. But when you give to the needy, do not let your left hand know what your right hand is doing, so that your giving may be in secret. Then your Father, who sees what is

done in secret, will reward you (Matt. 6:1-4).

After immediate needs have been attended to, opportunity should be provided for unemployed members of the church family to meet with each other. The group should focus on:

• discussing budget management and ways of adjusting to a lower standard of living during unemployment;

• understanding the changing job market in our country and in the immediate area;

• helping individuals define the nature of their gifts and skills;

• discovering the opportunities available for job training and retraining;

• informing the group of the availability of grants, low-interest loans and other forms of financial aid;

• identifying services available for job placement.

Through the effective ministry of Christian care groups such as these, the church can have a practical role in the redemption and restoration of the family of God. Even more exciting is the challenge of creating programs that can prevent unnecessary problems.

Suggested Readings—Chapters Seven and Eight

Debbie Barr, *Caught in the Crossfire* (Zondervan, 1985).

Gary Collins, *How to Be a People Helper* (Vision House, 1976).

Bea Decker, as told to Gladys Kooiman, *After the Flowers Have Gone* (Zondervan Publishing House, 1980).

Gerard Egan, *Interpersonal Living* (Belmont, Calif.: Wadsworth Publishing Company Inc., 1976).

Isabel Fleece, *Not by Accident: Comfort in Times of Loss* (Moody, 1987).

Jan Frank, *A Door of Hope* (San Bernardino, Calif.: Here's Life Publishers, 1987).

Janet Ohlemacher, *Beloved Alcoholic: What to Do When a Family Member Drinks* (Zondervan, 1984).

Sue Richards and Stanley Hagemeyer, *Ministry to the Divorced: Guidance, Structure and Organization That Promote Healing in the Church* (Zondervan, 1986).

Karl Slaikeu and Steve Lawhead, *The Phoenix Factor: Surviving and Growing Through Personal Crisis* (Zondervan, 1987).

Anderson Spickard and Barbara Thompson, *Dying for a Drink* (Word Books, 1985).

Pam Vredevelt and Joyce Whitman, *Walking a Thin Line: Anorexia and Bulimia—The Battle Can Be Won* (Multnomah Press, 1985).

Warren and David Wiersbe, *Comforting the Bereaved* (Moody, 1985).

Earl D. Wilson, *A Silence to Be Broken: Hope for Those Caught in the Web of Incest* (Multnomah, 1986).

Preventive Programs: Young People

Many problems don't need to happen. Often they result from inadequate or inaccurate information and lack of skill or control in decision making. Unwanted pregnancies, unwise marriages, drug abuse, dropping out of school, overspending, extramarital affairs, physical and emotional abuse, drunkenness, disappointing careers—these kinds of problems with all of the pain they entail are avoidable in many cases.

The church invests heavily in helping people survive the spiritual, emotional and social consequences of these problems. But, with only a little more effort than is being expended now, many of these problems can be prevented. In fact, the institutional church, through its departmental structure, is ideally suited for the implementation of programs that, over a person's life span, can help him or her avoid many painful problems.

In addition, by offering people information about healthy spiritual and emotional development and by teaching them appropriate skills for implementing this information, the church can have an effective ministry in helping its members maximize their divine potential.

Caution!

Before considering specific preventive programs, I want to remind you that the wall of separation between church and state is rapidly eroding. This increases the risks of legal liability in the event someone believes they or their children have been harmed on the property of the church or through its programs. The risk is particularly high in programs involving infants, toddlers, elementary school children and young people.

In order to protect the church against liability you should:

• Be sure that those responsible for the physical custody of children are trained adequately in safety procedures.

• Be sure you have a personnel file for each of your paid and volunteer staff members who are involved in children and youth programs.

• Be sure to include in each personnel file two or three references from people who know the person to be of sound Christian character and know of no reason they would pose a risk for children or young people.

• Be sure you have adequate insurance coverage.

Double-check your insurance policy for any exclusionary clauses.

Infants and Toddlers

People who work in the nursery should be selected carefully and trained thoroughly in handling infants and toddlers. Since this staff will change continually, training in these areas will need to be conducted regularly. Workers need to be taught that in addition to the service they are performing for the parents, they are also having a very meaningful ministry to the children themselves. Let me explain.

The baby's brain associates pleasure and pain with people and places. Thus the baby identifies the people and places representing risks and rewards in his or her life. To observe this, all you have to do is watch mothers bring their babies to a pediatrician's office. The doctor may have done everything possible to make the office pleasant for children, but the child's brain will not let him forget the painful shots he gets there. On the other hand, going up the steps to Grandma's house excites an altogether different response.

We want the baby to associate pleasure with the place called God's house and with the people he or she will later identify as God's family. Affectionate handling, hugs and smiles will help build this kind of association.

Be sure to include men among your nursery workers. Most children of single and divorced mothers are seldom held by men. Contact with a healthy male, even for the short time the youngster is in the church nursery, can make a positive contribution to the child's view of adult men.

Senior high school students are often mature enough to work in the nursery if they are adequately trained. Allowing young people to experience some of the responsibility of child care may help them understand more clearly the serious risks of being sexually active before marriage and make them more inclined to wait.

Choosing an Occupation

Can you imagine what your church would be like if each young person grew up with a healthy understanding of the theology of work? Through our work we manifest God's gifts to us. In our work place we reach those to whom He has called us with the witness of our lives.

In Genesis, Moses reveals God as a worker, creating the heavens and the earth. God brings His work week to an end by making man in His own image and by giving him a job to do. God intends for His mission in our lives to be carried on through the work He has gifted us to do.

First-century Christians expressed God's plan for their lives in their occupations. Early Christians represented diverse walks of life. Some were fishermen, while others were carpenters, tax collectors, physicians, merchants, tentmakers, lawyers or metalsmiths (see Matt. 13:53-55; Luke 19:1-8; John 21:1-14; Acts 16:14, 18:1-3; Col. 4:14; 2 Tim. 4:14; Titus 3:13).

A few were called to leave their occupations and devote their lives to preparing others for the ministry of world evangelism (see Eph. 4:11-13). However, most of them found the call of God expressed in their lives by sharing Christ with others through their vocational gifts.

In his letter to the Romans, Paul urges Christians to discover and develop their vocational gifts as expressions of their stewardship of God's grace.

> Therefore, I urge you, brothers, in view of God's mercy, to offer your bodies as living sacrifices, holy and pleasing to God—this is your spiritual act of worship. Do not conform any longer to the pattern of this world, but be transformed by the renewing of your mind. Then you will be able to test and approve what God's will is—His good, pleasing and perfect will.
>
> For by the grace given me I say to every one of you: Do not think of yourself more highly than you ought, but rather think of yourself with sober judgment, in accordance with the measure of faith God has given you. Just as each of us has one body with many members, and these members do not all have the same function, so in Christ we who are many form one body, and each member belongs to all the others. We have different gifts, according to the grace given us. If a man's gift is prophesying, let him use it in proportion to his faith. If it is serving, let him serve; if it is teaching, let him teach; if it is encouraging, let him encourage; if it is contributing to the needs of others, let him give generously; if it is leadership, let him govern diligently; if it is showing mercy, let him do

it cheerfully (Rom. 12:1-8).

Occupation or Vocation?

Traditionally, the church has restricted the use of the word "calling" almost exclusively to the professional clergy. This leaves the average parishioner feeling that God is not concerned with what he or she does for a living. Nothing could be further from the truth.

We are all called into the body of Christ. Although some of us are called to the clergy, with the primary task of preparing others for the work of the ministry, we are all called to be ministers. We discover the people to whom we are called through the expression of our vocational gifts.

Today, many Christian parents split their lives artificially into secular and sacred spheres. From Monday to Friday and often Saturday they give their employers their work time; on Sunday they go to church and give God His time. Their concept of stewardship is limited to tithing and an occasional offering.

Such a concept of the Christian faith neatly compartmentalizes life into what is "God's" and what is "mine." Young people raised in such families are likely to continue this pattern. Implicit in the New Testament concept of stewardship, however, is the acknowledgment that all we have belongs to God and none of it belongs to us.

> Jesus told His disciples: "There was a rich man whose manager was accused of wasting his possessions. So he called him in and asked him,

'What is this I hear about you? Give an account of your management, because you cannot be manager any longer' '' (Luke 16:1-2).

So then, men ought to regard us as servants of Christ and as those entrusted with the secret things of God. Now it is required that those who have been given a trust must prove faithful (1 Cor. 4:1-2).

Each one should use whatever gift he has received to serve others, faithfully administering God's grace in its various forms (1 Pet. 4:10).

We Are All Ministers

How can we help the family of God recapture the New Testament sense of stewardship and calling in relation to their work? I suggest we begin with a concentrated emphasis on vocational choice. This would involve devoting a fifteen-minute segment of the Christian education hour every two months to the task of acquainting children with people who have captured the vision of stewardship through their vocation.

The people chosen to participate in this program need to be coached in what to say. If the concept of stewardship is to be communicated successfully, three thoughts are critical to the success of the program:

• Our primary purpose in life is to serve God and His people wherever we are.

• God has given unique vocational gifts to every boy and girl. These gifts can be discovered by observing the things we enjoy doing and can do well. The sooner in life we discover our gifts, the more likely we are to develop them fully.

• We are all ministers. We are not all pastors, but we are all ministers. The purpose of the minister is to serve and to share the love of Christ with people we meet through our work. Fulfilling this purpose brings dignity and meaning to the most menial task and provides the humility necessary for combatting the pride and arrogance of professionalism.

Of course, what is said will need to be put into the language of the age group being addressed. But here is an example of what one might say:

I suppose as children all of us wonder what we will do when we grow up. Unless someone tells us, we may not know that God is really more interested in what we do during the week than He is in what we do on Sunday. Because it is what we do through the week that brings us in contact with people who have not yet discovered how much Jesus loves them. He knows that each of us can communicate His love to some people more effectively than we can to others. The people we can best reach are those we contact through our vocational gifts. God is concerned about our financial needs, and if we pursue excellence in what we do, these physical needs will be met. But we should always remember that our primary purpose in life is to share the love of Christ with those around us.

When should such a program begin? Why not begin with four-year-olds? After all, this is the time boys and girls begin to play grown-up. They put on their parents' clothes, pretend to be married, go to work, and so on.

At this stage in life, boys and girls think very concretely. Therefore, the people participating in the program should be from vocations that require some kind of uniform—nurses, policemen, firemen, mechanics, doctors, carpenters, lab technicians, dentists.

Once youngsters are in first grade they begin to think more abstractly. The range of occupations represented in the program can be broadened. Care should be taken to include women in a wide variety of vocations—including homemaking.

If this program is followed carefully, youngsters who are introduced to it at age four and continue through their senior year of high school will have had an opportunity to sample a wide range of vocations.

The networking possibilities of such a program are almost unlimited. For example, early in life, adults will be introduced to the vocational interests of children and will be able to encourage them. Young adults will find among church members in their chosen vocational field Christian models who can help them with job placement.

With such a program in place young people are more likely to make a smooth transition from childhood to adulthood. Experience with teenagers reveals that those who are committed to vocational goals early in life are much less likely to be involved with drugs or the complications of teenage pregnancy.

Choosing Friends

"A man of many companions may come to ruin, but there is a friend who sticks closer than a brother" (Prov. 18:24). Outside our family, there is no greater influence upon our lives than the friends we choose.

Remember David and Jonathan? The bond of love between them was stronger than that between Jonathan and his own father, Saul. There are times in the lives of most young people when their friendship ties are stronger than their family ties. A poor choice of friends has been the ruination of many. Yet, at the same time, a wise choice of friends can be our salvation.

Young people need to learn the importance of the environment in which they find their friends. Something so obvious to older people has not yet dawned upon the young. Certain kinds of places attract certain kinds of people. You're not likely to find a good Christian friend at the local bar.

Among the safest places for young people to discover wholesome friendships are their church, their school and their neighborhood. What makes these places safe? They are more accessible to parents. Friendships formed there are more easily monitored.

Of course, even these environments are not risk free. Unfortunately, some friendships formed among young people in the church can be disastrous. This is why parents should know the families from which their children choose their friends. Family characteristics are the most critical variable in determining the safety of friendships.

Young people often confuse their Christian obligation to befriend everyone with their personal responsibility for choosing their close friends wisely. They can be helped in making this difficult distinction by being reminded that there are various kinds of friends.

Jesus demonstrates this distinction in choosing His friends. A careful look at His relationships with people reveals that He reserved more time for those who chose His way of life, and He shared more intimate experiences with them than He did with the multitudes.

First of all, Jesus chose seventy to help Him preach and heal. Then He chose the Twelve to be closer to Him in ministry. From those He chose three to be His closest friends: He took Peter, James and John with Him when He healed Jairus' daughter; they were also with Him on the Mount of Transfiguration and in the Garden of Gethsemane. Of these, John was the most intimate friend of Jesus. He leaned on His breast at the Last Supper and against His cross at the time of His crucifixion.

Types of Friendships

In much the same manner each of us builds friendships that vary in degrees of intimacy. We have casual friends whom we often see in our daily lives, but we only get to know them in superficial ways. Passing the time of day with them is pleasant, but that is all we share. Christians should be able to be casual friends with most of those they meet.

Recreational friends are people we meet for fun and games—tennis, racquetball, golf, party games, and so on. When the recreation we share with them is over, we part company until we meet to play again.

Then there are friends we study with—academic friends. We help each other prepare for exams. But when school is over, we seldom see each other.

Each of us needs two or three close friends with whom

we can share our innermost thoughts. These friends may be among those involved in the other activities mentioned. But they should also share our faith since they have a far more important role in our lives. They help us get through the rough times with less pain and celebrate the good times with more joy. These are the people we think of calling first when we are hurting or have good news to share. Our close friends love us enough to challenge us when our views of life are extreme and to encourage us when life overwhelms us.

In early adolescence our closest friends are likely to be members of the same sex. However, in middle and late adolescence, they may include members of the opposite sex.

Friendship Skills

In order to be comfortable in making friends, young people need to learn simple conversational skills. Certainly, learning to introduce yourself to others and engaging in "small talk" are helpful. Although people frequently voice their frustration concerning the role small talk plays at social gatherings, who is willing to risk talking about personal matters with someone until they are comfortable with that person in general conversation?

Loyalty is also an essential friendship skill. If teenagers are going to build healthy friendships, they must learn how to be loyal to their friends.

Friends must also learn to love unselfishly and to forgive. No healthy friendship is one-sided. Healthy friends know how to give and receive love. And they know how to put their differences in the past.

Jesus was a master of these basic friendship skills. Remember His meeting with the woman at the well of Samaria? He talked about a common topic—water—in putting her at ease with Him. He talked about fish with fishermen and about taxes with tax collectors. And who can question His loyalty, love and forgiveness to His friends? "Greater love has no one than this, that He lay down His life for His friends" (John 15:13).

Helping young people learn friendship skills is an important ministry in preparing them to enjoy a useful and effective Christian life. By providing a special emphasis on Christian friendship skills for junior high and senior high youngsters, we can prevent many of the far-reaching risks of ill-chosen relationships. Such a program should extend over a number of weeks and should be offered at both age levels. This can be done through either the Christian education or youth departments of the church.

Preventive Programs: Marriage and Family Life

Until recently, young people were usually able to look to their parents as healthy models of marriage and family life. However, since so many of our children today grow up in broken homes, parents may no longer be the most reliable models. Where else can young people look for help in this important area? Outside the family, the church is the only institution that can provide both the information and value structure necessary for a stable marital foundation. Here again, the family of God has an opportunity to assume a role neglected by many natural families.

Choosing a Partner

The Christian education and youth departments are ideally suited to provide junior and senior high students with training in this vitally important area. The first class should be offered in the eighth grade when young people are beginning to think seriously about how they are perceived by the opposite sex. The second class should be offered in the eleventh grade before most of them have seriously committed themselves to a relationship.

What should these classes address? Certainly these classes should familiarize young people with a Christian mate selection system. They also should make young people aware of the boundaries between various levels of physical contact in a dating relationship. A strong emphasis should be placed on the biblical principles involved in mate selection.

Unfortunately, many young people do not even know about a Christian mate selection process. When they know the process they are much less likely to be victimized by it.

A balanced mate selection process actually begins with the *initial dating experience*. This is where a young person begins to develop the skills for becoming acquainted with a member of the opposite sex.

The second stage finds young people beginning to date a number of partners. This *random dating* stage is the most important phase of the process. By noticing the positive and negative characteristics of each dating partner, a young man or woman develops an imaginary composite of the ideal dating partner. This is refined with each new experience and can be used as a mental frame of reference for the eventual mate choice.

The third stage we refer to as *going steady*. The purpose here is to test the partners' ability to be faithful to the relationship and to see how satisfying the relationship remains over a period of time. Marriage requires both.

The fourth stage is referred to as *pre-engagement*. This period begins with an informal understanding between the partners that they intend to get married. At this stage, family and friends are not informed. It is the couple's secret.

Engagement is the fifth stage. Traditionally, this begins with the male asking the father of his girlfriend for permission to marry her. Ideally, the engagement period will extend from six months to two years. Studies indicate that engagement periods shorter or longer than this are negatively correlated with success in marriage.

Young people should understand that the purpose of the engagement period is to give them one last opportunity to opt out of the relationship before marriage. Even though breaking the relationship at this stage is painful, broken engagements do not hurt nearly as much as broken marriages.

Physical Contact in Dating

From the time young people begin to date until they get married, they are faced with the challenge of controlling the physical dimensions of their relationships. Overcommitment to the physical dimensions of love is probably the most frequent precipitating factor in unwise mate choices.

145

Such unwise choices usually result from the unconscious operation of an informal process known as the double-funnel theory of mate selection. This is how it works. Young men want contact. Young women want commitment. When the young man makes a little commitment, he wants more contact. When the young woman gives more contact, she wants more commitment. The farther down this "funnel of love" the couple goes, the more slippery the funnel becomes. The next thing a couple knows, they are married—and they are not quite sure at what point in their trip down the funnel they ever decided to get married.

Marriage is too important to back into like this. Such a lifetime commitment should be made carefully and prayerfully.

Biblical Principles in Mate Selection

The spiritual qualities of a person's character should be the first consideration in mate choice. Whether one looks at the Old Testament or the New Testament, Scripture places great importance on marrying within your faith tradition. Jews were not permitted to intermarry with others from pagan religions. Christians were required to marry Christians.

> Do not be yoked together with unbelievers. For what do righteousness and wickedness have in common? Or what fellowship can light have with darkness? What harmony is there between Christ and Belial? What does a believer have in common with an unbeliever? What agreement is

there between the temple of God and idols? For we are the temple of the living God. As God has said: "I will live with them and walk among them, and I will be their God, and they will be my people. Therefore come out from them and be separate," says the Lord. "Touch no unclean thing, and I will receive you. I will be a Father to you, and you will be my sons and daughters, says the Lord Almighty" (2 Cor. 6:14-18).

Care should also be taken to consider the compatibility of the groom's family and the bride's family. Abraham and Sarah went to great lengths to see that Isaac had a bride from their own tribe. This tradition was also followed by Jacob in choosing Rachel. Young people need to know that marriage not only unites two people, it unites two families. A marriage that brings together two compatible families is much more likely to succeed than one that ignores this aspect.

Material suited for use in preparing young people for mate selection can be found in my videotape and booklet *Narrowing the Risk in Mate Selection* (Emerge Ministries).

Training for Marriage

Very few people enter into marriage with an understanding of the skills necessary to succeed in it. To make matters worse, most newlyweds have highly unrealistic expectations of marriage. When couples don't know the skills required to succeed in marriage and enter it with unrealistic expectations, they can easily find themselves headed for an unwanted and unwarranted divorce.

Not only is the institution of the family affected by such unnecessary tragedies, the church is also devastated by them. After all, no church is stronger than the families that form it. And no family is stronger than the marriage on which it is built.

So why shouldn't the church offer engaged couples an opportunity to gain a knowledge of the skills marriage requires and provide them with a realistic picture of marriage? In the same program, couples can be reminded of the stark contrast between secular and Christian marriages. This will give them a head start in building strong and healthy families.

The adult Christian education department provides a convenient setting in which an annual class on training for marriage might meet. In larger churches (five hundred or more), such a class might meet twice a year, in the spring and fall. By requiring all engaged couples to attend, the pastor's premarital counseling duties can be reduced considerably.

This class should define realistic expectations for couples entering marriage. It should also teach the skills required of couples who would succeed in marriage. Experts agree that skills in care giving, communication, problem solving and conflict resolution are essential in building long-lasting marriages.

A developmental view of marriage will go a long way toward informing couples of what lies ahead of them. If they have children, their marriage will flow through five rather well-defined stages: *adjustment*, *childbearing*, *child rearing*, *child launching* and *empty nest*.

Understanding the characteristics and concerns of each of these stages will help couples correct unrealistic expectations and prevent unnecessary disappointments.

Training for Parenthood

Just as many couples assume that getting married automatically endows them with the skills to succeed in marriage, many parents assume that the experience of having a baby brings with it the knowledge and skills for parenthood. This kind of logic would lead one to conclude that buying an automobile automatically endows you with the skills to drive and repair it.

The beginning of parenthood presents a couple with the greatest opportunity for providing a healthy future for their children. However, very few parents give themselves or their children the benefits of formal training in parenting. Yet the Bible admonishes us to "train a child in the way he should go" and promises that, if we do, "when he is old he will not turn from it" (Prov. 22:6).

Everything the behavioral sciences have learned about the growth and development of children confirms the tremendous impact early training has on character and behavior in later years. This underscores the need for the church to be involved in training Christian parents for this life-shaping responsibility.

In my film and videotape series *Building Families That Last* (Emerge Ministries), I describe what I call the five essential characteristics of a successful Christian family. They are *love and affection*; *cooperation*; *communication*; *discipline*; and *forgiveness*. Children need to be introduced to an environment that manifests these characteristics. As they grow up, they need to acquire the skills necessary for expressing them in their relationships with others.

In order to communicate effectively with their children, parents need to learn how to get into their children's world. In the course of raising a child, parents must learn to translate their thoughts into five different levels of communication: the *preverbal* world of the infant, the *concrete and functional* worlds of the preschooler, the *simple abstract* world of the elementary school child, the *private and abstract* world of the early adolescent, and the *morally sophisticated* world of the later adolescent. Pointing out these language differences will clarify much of the confusion in parenthood.

Discipline

Parents are primarily charged with the responsibility of disciplining their children. Discipline is simply training for living. Many parents mistake punishment for discipline. You can punish a child without disciplining him, but you cannot discipline him without punishing him.

Punishment is designed to discourage undesirable behavior by inflicting physical and/or emotional pain. However, discipline consists of forming desirable behavior in a child.

It is possible to teach a child what he or she is *not* supposed to do without teaching the child what he or she *is* supposed to do. Children raised in this way bring this same mindset to their faith as adults. They are better able to articulate what Christians are not supposed to do than they are to describe what Christians are supposed to do. They have a punitive view of their faith rather than a rewarding view. Their God is more a God of wrath than a God of love.

However, when children are taught what they ought to do (which is the purpose of healthy discipline), they experience the rewards of a disciplined life. And when they come to know the Lord, they are more likely to see the benefits of the Christian life.

Since the skills required for parenting preschool, preteen and teenage children are very different, separate classes should be provided for the parents of these various age groups. My books *Venturing Into a Child's World* (Revell) and *Venturing Into a Teenager's World* (Revell) are organized into thirteen chapters for use in quarterly Christian education programs. Videotape series are also available for each of these books.

ELEVEN

Preventive Programs: Mid-life and Beyond

Probably the two most stress-filled decades of life are the forties and fifties. Yet few people are prepared to face them.

What makes these years so trying? For the first time, parents experience powerlessness in their efforts to protect their children. Then, while our children are marrying, many of us are burying our parents, which confronts us with our own mortality. As though this were not enough, during this same period, our careers are peaking and the end of our work life is in sight. Is it any wonder that the stress of mid-life takes a toll on marriage and health?

Although there is no way to eliminate all the stress

associated with these drastic changes, knowing what is ahead and being able to prepare for it can certainly reduce the severity of its impact. The church has much to gain from helping people prepare for mid-life.

Parenting in Mid-life

When children are small and unable to think in complex, abstract terms, they are no physical or mental match for their parents. This makes them relatively easy to control. However, when the burst of adolescent growth occurs and the abstracting ability of teenagers allows them to challenge their parents mentally, parents feel more and more powerless.

Regulating the tension between the freedom teenagers want and the restrictions they need becomes more difficult. Often, the desire that insecure parents have for their children's love leads to further aggravation: there are times when children feel that they have the most unfair and unreasonable parents in the world. At times like these, parents need help.

Educating children in today's world can put a sizeable financial strain on the family. Churches that help parents plan ahead for this difficult time are rendering an invaluable service to their families.

Anyone who has launched young people into marriage knows how stressful this is. First of all, anxiety arises over your child's choice of a mate. Even if you feel the choice is unwise, you can put only so much pressure on your son or daughter to change it. Then the expense of a wedding is no small matter (even if it is your son who is getting married!). In addition to all this, parents are bound to feel an emotional loss when their children marry. It is the rare church that helps the family anticipate these things so they can prepare for them spiritually and emotionally.

Dealing With the Loss of Parents

People in mid-life often feel they are parenting two generations—their children and their parents. When parents' health begins to fail, children feel the need to assume more and more care for them. More often than not, this occurs in our forties and fifties.

Sometimes it is necessary to bring aging parents into the home. When this occurs, usually everyone feels the pressure. After all, more people have to share the telephones, bathrooms and other living conveniences. Grandparents often have difficulty allowing parents to manage the family ("their grandchildren") without interference. Children may also feel that their parents have become stricter since the grandparents moved in.

More stress is created when parents are incapacitated and must be placed in a nursing home. Even when the parents choose to go to the nursing home, many children suffer guilt from seeing them there. Watching the health of parents fail is traumatic. Not only do children feel helpless in sparing their parents from suffering, but they are confronted with the inevitability of their own death.

The Work World

At mid-life, if a person is not reaching or nearing his or her career goals, it is time for reassessment. Burying dreams that are obviously not attainable brings a sense of loss and grief.

For those who are at their career peaks, realizing that future promotions are limited can lessen motivation for external goals and result in a more reflective attitude toward life. For them, there may be more and more emphasis on "smelling the roses."

Regardless of whether you are burying dreams or smelling roses, mid-life takes its toll. Divorce rates skyrocket; heart attacks claim their greatest number of victims; suicides peak—people in mid-life are crying out for help. What a challenge for the church!

A class helping those in mid-life to understand and deal with their specific challenges can also be a very effective evangelistic tool. There is no better time to introduce people to Christ and a better way of life than when they are struggling with painful mid-life crises.

Preparing for Retirement

Sometimes nature exhibits more wisdom than we human beings do in planning for the future. Solomon suggests that the ant can teach us some valuable lessons in preparing for retirement.

> Go to the ant, you sluggard; consider its ways
> and be wise! It has no commander, no overseer
> or ruler, yet it stores its provisions in summer
> and gathers its food at harvest (Prov. 6:6-8).

People in their early forties should have the opportunity of attending a class designed to help them prepare for retirement. Since most people this young are reluctant to think about retirement, such a class may benefit from a topic like "Making the Most of Your Future."

Among the things to be considered in such a class are adopting a healthy diet and exercise program; taking steps necessary to maintain a healthy marriage; establishing adequate savings; and developing hobbies and interests in addition to one's work.

In preparing for retirement, people need to be reminded of the Christian virtue of temperance. Extremes in life are seldom good for anyone.

This is especially true of diet and exercise programs. Unsound diet and exercise fads can be fatal. Life becomes more sedentary for most of us as we grow older. Knowing what this means in terms of calorie intake and the muscle tone of the body helps motivate people to make the necessary adjustments. Getting competent professional guidance in these areas is important.

Retirement often brings to married couples the surprising discovery that being around each other for long periods of time is not as blissful as anticipated. This is especially true for couples who have neglected to enrich their marriage through the years. So, in preparing couples for retirement, a class like this should remind them of healthy spiritual priorities: God, spouse, family, work, church, friends and community.

As parenting responsibilities decrease and work goals diminish, couples have more time for each other. Helping them plan creatively for this time together is an important ministry of the church.

Another critical consideration is money. Studies

indicate that people who are able to maintain their standard of living into retirement are healthier, happier and live longer. Making such preparation should be considered a part of good stewardship. Here again, people need to be urged to seek sound professional advice.

The specter of catastrophic illness lurks in the minds of most older people. The only way to prepare adequately for such an eventuality is through a comprehensive insurance program. The average person will need help in understanding the "small print" in many insurance policies. Simply teaching people the critical questions to ask their insurance carriers and where to look in their policies for possible flaws can prevent much mental anguish and unnecessary financial hardship.

Often people become too consumed by parenting and their careers to develop the additional interests necessary to make retirement inviting. Acquainting them with, and urging them to become active in, various community agencies can help them discover ways they can enrich their lives and extend the ministry of the church.

The benefits of mid-life career changes can also be explored in this class. This does not necessarily mean moving to a totally unrelated field. People often find other jobs within the same occupation that give them a new challenge.

Concluding Remarks

At the heart of the healing ministry of Jesus is the goal of spiritual wholeness for the entire Christian family. After all, we are all members of His body.

The greatest challenge facing the American church

today is the broken family. So it was in Jesus' day. The first-century church offered broken families hope—hope for spiritual wholeness through its caring community. In fact, the early church became a surrogate spiritual family for the lonely and oppressed.

Again today, the lonely and oppressed are crying out for help and hope. Today's church must resist the temptation to succumb to bureaucratic and impersonal methods of ministry. We must meet the needs of the broken modern family.

Through the careful planning and implementation of both preventive and redemptive ministries, the church can utilize its departmental structure to care for the family of God.

Suggested Readings—Chapters Nine, Ten and Eleven

John Q. Baucom, *Help Your Children Say No to Drugs* (Zondervan, 1987).

Garry Friesen, *Decision Making and the Will of God: A Biblical Alternative to the Traditional View* (Multnomah, 1981).

Christopher Carstens and William Mahedy, *Starting on Monday: Christian Living in the Workplace* (Ballantine, 1987).

Jim and Sally Conway, *Women in Mid-Life Crisis* (Nelson, 1987).

THE FAMILY-FRIENDLY CHURCH

Bud and Kathy Pearson, *Single Again: Remarrying for the Right Reasons* (Regal, 1985).

Jerry E. and Mary A. White, *Your Job: Survival or Satisfaction* (Zondervan, 1977).

Emerge Ministries is a center for the treatment and prevention of mental health problems. The center offers seminars and training programs on marriage and family counseling, personal development and other topics of concern to pastors and counselors. Books, tapes, and film and video series on mental health can be obtained through the ministry, and a professional staff is available for counseling.

For further information, please contact:

Emerge Ministries
900 Mull Avenue
Akron, OH 44313
(216) 867-5603

For a listing of other Creation House books, write to:

190 N. Westmonte Drive
Altamonte Springs, FL 32714